T0160829

Advent to Epiphany

Advent to Epiphany

Engaging the Heart of Christmas

An Interactive Devotional

From Friends:
Liena Apšukrapša & Jacqueline L. Hullaby

Carpenter's Son Publishing

Advent to Epiphany
Engaging the True Heart of Christmas

Copyright © 2016 Liena Apšukrapša & Jacqueline L. Hullaby

All rights reserved.

978-1-946889-49-2

No part of this work may be reproduced or transmitted in any form or by any means, electronic or mechanical, including photocopying and recording, or by any information storage or retrieval system, except as may be expressly permitted by the 1976 Copyright Act or in writing from the authors.

All Scripture quotations, unless otherwise indicated, are taken from the Holy Bible, New International Version®. NIV®. Copyright © 1973, 1978, 1984, 2011 by Biblica, Inc.™ Used by permission of Zondervan. All rights reserved worldwide. www.zondervan.com. The "NIV" and "New International Version" are trademarks registered in the United States Patent and Trademark office by Biblica, Inc.™

Scripture quotations marked KJV are taken from the King James Version of the Bible.

Scripture quotations marked (NLT) are taken from the *Holy Bible, New Living Translation,* copyright © 1996, 2004, 2007, 2013 by Tyndale House Foundation. Used by permission of Tyndale House Publishers, Inc., Carol Stream, Illinois 60188. All rights reserved.

Scripture quotations marked NASB are taken from the New American Standard Bible®, Copyright © 1960, 1962, 1963, 1968, 1971, 1972, 1973, 1975, 1977, 1995 by The Lockman Foundation. Used by permission.

Scripture quotations marked AMP are taken from *The Amplified® Bible,* Copyright © 1954, 1958, 1962, 1964, 1965, 1987, by The Lockman Foundation. Used by permission. (www.Lockman.org.) All rights reserved.

Dedicated to Friendship

"There is nothing on this earth more to be prized than true friendship."
Thomas Aquinas

Contents

A Note to Our Readers

"Here I am!" says Jesus expectantly. "I stand at the door and knock. If anyone hears my voice and opens the door, I will come in" (Revelation 3:20). Will you satisfy His desire and invite Him to commune with you this Advent and Christmas?

Jesus is coming to us, but He wants us to move toward Him. So it is a season of our advent as well—a bold emerging into the presence of God.

Our intent is to host your encounter with Jesus involving your entire person: mind, soul, senses, imagination, and spirit. We believe He longs to raise you up to a new level of relating to Him, to yourself, and to the world around you.

This devotional is not academic by nature, but rather it invites you to enter into the stories surrounding Jesus' birth accompanied by your internal guide, the Holy Spirit. Henri Nouwen, an internationally renowned priest and author, writes, "One of the remarkable qualities of the story is that it creates space. We can dwell in a story, walk around, and find our own place. The story confronts but does not oppress; the story inspires but does not manipulate. The story invites us to an encounter, a dialog, a mutual sharing. The story brings us into touch with the vision and so guides us." [*The Living Reminder: Service and Prayer in Reminder of Jesus Christ*] We believe this is the reason the story is so prevalent in the Scriptures.

We pray and hope this will be a meaningful experience for you with the Lord and will lead you to your own epiphany.

Let's journey together!
Liena and Jacqueline

The First Week of Advent

Living with a Paradox

Dear Advent Pilgrim,

What a great paradox: God becomes a baby and a servant to us all. Seemingly absurd, but so necessary. Our lives are filled with paradoxes. Just look around. Are you or someone close to you young but dying, desiring a family but single, talented but jobless, nurturing but barren, married but lonely? How do we live with these paradoxes—not only live but thrive in the midst of them? Today's reading takes us directly to a paradox in Elizabeth and Zechariah's lives. Come and explore with us.

Preparing to Reflect

Prayer and reflection is a sacred and set-apart time for communion with God. It is helpful to create a special place to meet with Him daily. As I am about to start my Advent journey and this time of prayer, how do I find myself? I get in touch with my heart. Am I expectant, thirsty, content, frustrated, or maybe weary? I pause and take few deep breaths. I bring my true self before God and welcome what He desires to give me today.

Prayer

Lord, surprise me with Your goodness this Advent season and always. Amen.

Story of the Day

In the time of Herod king of Judea there was a priest named Zechariah, who belonged to the priestly division of Abijah; his wife Elizabeth was also a descendant of Aaron. Both of them were righteous in the sight of God, observing all the Lord's commands and decrees blamelessly. But they were childless because Elizabeth was not able to conceive, and they were both very old (Luke 1:5–7).

Entering the Scene

Come and enter this couple's life. If you were to live with Elizabeth and Zechariah for a while, what would you notice about them? What rumors would you hear about this elderly couple?

At a glance, they have it all. The couple comes from a prominent priestly line. They have been married a long time, are respected in their community, and have a lovely home and servants. Not only that, their walk with God is blameless.

But there is a huge immovable elephant in their room. They can't have children. Nobody will continue the family line.

Do you know people in this predicament, or maybe you are one of them?

The entire community is bewildered in light of the common belief of their time that barrenness is a punishment from God. The unanswerable questions circulate around like obnoxious flies: "How come Zechariah and Elizabeth are so righteous but God has punished them with barrenness? What's the reason?"

Sadly Zechariah and Elizabeth are living with a great paradox that's not going away. The expectation of having children has slowly dimmed with each year. Now not only is Elizabeth barren, they also are both old. Their angst and desire to have children are so deeply buried in their hearts, they don't visit it any longer. It's too painful and too late. With time the river of hope has dried up. The bedrock, however, is still there. Will new healing waters arise?

Going Deeper

What paradoxes are there in your life? What things do you wrestle with that don't seem to make sense?

Elizabeth and Zechariah have struggled for a long time, but they continue their faithful walk with God in spite of the ball of disgrace attached to them with an invisible chain.

Do you know someone whose faith is unwavering despite deep tragedies, unmet dreams, and profound losses?

In my work as a chaplain I, Liena, have worked with countless people in the midst of intense suffering. There is a common note I hear in the hearts of mature believers that pierces through the darkness of devastation. It's the note of faith in the boundless goodness of God. This is also the music we hear in Elizabeth's and Zechariah's hearts. In the absence of the desired gift of a child, they still uphold the abundance of the Giver's many gifts.

Devotion and humility have created a protective space around their hearts to withstand the external pressure of paradox. In that space God is creating a miracle with a smile on His face. Maybe things are not, after all, as they appear to be. What has been considered a curse might be a blessing. God's implicit message to the elderly couple is a tender reminder of His greatness. "What you consider the devastation of barrenness and old age is the most fruitful soil for My miracles and might."

Pope Francis's words ring true: "You must leave room for the Lord, not for our certainties; we must be humble." True humility is a profound openness to what we don't yet know. A humble and wise heart lives with the relentless expectation of God's goodness. Humbleness always leaves one's heart receptive to vast possibilities and lets Jesus be Lord. This is the true Advent invitation for you and also for us.

Prayer for the Journey

Lord, thank You for being ever present and surprising in all my circumstances. I long to see my reality with Your eyes and through Your Holy Spirit. Keep my heart open to what I don't know yet. Amen.

Your Response

Ponder for a moment how God might help you to see your paradoxes in a new light. Bring this to the Lord in prayer. Journal your thoughts as a letter to Him.

Your loving Advent friends,
Liena and Jacqueline

I Remember You

Dear Friend,

What is the sweetest way in which someone has remembered you? Think for a moment. Isn't there something particularly heart-warming about the intentionality of this act of love?

In today's story God remembers an old man and woman in a way that completely changes their lives. Let's see how!

Preparing to Reflect

I settle down and recollect myself before God. "And what is recollection? A combination of two things: first, a state of release of tension, relaxation, receptivity; second, a state of attentiveness to a reality toward which we are totally orientated." [Jacques Philippe, *Thirsting for Prayer*] Can I now become aware of any tension in my body and breathe deeply for few minutes to release it? I slowly turn my attention to the Lord who is waiting for me in love.

Prayer

"According to your love remember me, for you, LORD, are good" (Psalm 25:7). Amen.

Story of the Day

Once when Zechariah's division was on duty and he was serving as priest before God, he was chosen by lot, according to the custom of the priesthood, to go into the temple of the Lord and burn incense. And when the time for the burning of incense came, all the assembled worshipers were praying outside.

Then an angel of the Lord appeared to him, standing at the right side of the altar of incense. When Zechariah saw him, he was startled and was gripped with fear. But the angel said to him: "Do not be afraid, Zechariah; your prayer has been heard" (Luke 1:8–13).

Entering the Scene

The priests from the division of Abijah travel near and far for a very important event of casting lots. Who will be the elected priest to enter the Holy Place in the temple to burn incense on the altar? Guesses swirl like leaves in the autumn wind. What do you see, smell, hear, and notice in the midst of this holy hustle and bustle?

A priest could be chosen for this special duty only once in his lifetime. Zechariah has never been fortunate to be the one. The chances are decreasing with the passing years. Is he hoping but not quite believing anymore? Can you relate?

Bang, a striking surprise! Zechariah's heart leaps; God wants him for this duty after all.

Zechariah takes burning coals from the brazen altar of sacrifice out in the temple court. He places the incense upon them. A cloud of pungent aroma surrounds him as he slowly walks into the temple.

The prayers of the faithful in the temple court join the incense mounting up to the heavens. The voices rise and fall like the ebb and flow of the sea asking God to enter the Holy Place and accept with favor the offering of His people.

Zechariah places the incense on the beautiful acacia wood altar covered with a veneer of gold. The priest is about to rush away when a wall of light and glory hits his face. Is it an angel? Can it be true?

Steel-like fear grips the old man, and his legs grow weak. One thought takes over: "What have I done wrong?" And then the angel speaks.

Going Deeper

Zechariah is so surprised when an angel says to him: "God has heard your prayer." What prayer? He frantically searches his memory. The one prayed forty years ago? Ironically enough, Zechariah's name means "God (Jehovah) remembers."

The old priest is stunned. God has held in His memory that which has been too tender for Zechariah even to recall.

It's not a secret that the chambers of our heart hold many desires and prayers locked with keys that have been thrown away in disappointment many years ago.

The Scriptures give us countless other stories of God remembering someone in their distress like Rachel, Hannah, Abraham, Noah, and the nation of Israel.

God's remembering is always intertwined with His compassion toward us. I, Liena, would like to share a story of how God remembered my friend, David Michael Carrillo, who had a fruitful ministry of many years that suffered a demise.

Suddenly I was swept away by the flood of divine transition. I stopped in the middle of my walk, looked up to the heavens, and cried to the Lord, "Do you see me? Do you remember me?"

I recalled Genesis 8:1 where God remembered Noah. It wasn't that God forgot that Noah was floating adrift somewhere after the Great Flood. The word "remembered" in Hebrew means "to act on one's behalf out of love and concern" God made a promise to Noah to save him aboard the Ark. I wondered how Noah might have felt if he had never again seen dry land. I questioned if I even had a purpose in life again.

Nevertheless, God in His perfect timing brought the ark to rest on the mountain. Once the door opened, Noah and his family saw a completely new world and had a brand-new beginning.

As I waited on the Lord (and believe me, at times it was painful, confusing, and uncomfortable), He began to open new doors to a completely different life and ministry as a missionary serving in the country of Latvia.

Sometimes I just stand in awe when I look back, "Yes Lord, you did see me. Yes Lord, you know where I'm going in life. Thank you Lord for remembering me.

What are your forgotten prayers and deepest desires—the ones locked away but still burning in your heart as a perpetual angst? What are your stories of God remembering you?

Prayer for the Journey

My loving God, let me find an incredible peace and rest as I remember You always look at me and my heart's desires with great tenderness. Amen.

Your Response

At this moment, how do you need to be remembered by God? Offer your honest plea to God and journal your thoughts and prayers.

In prayer for you,
Your Advent companions

Great in God's Eyes

Christ's Beloved,

Can you recall a time in your life when you were utterly astonished by good news, something that sounded almost unbelievable?

Today we are about to witness Zechariah's surprise: a dream-like prophecy of an angel announcing the birth of a son. The angel tells Zechariah that his long-awaited gift will be "great in the sight of the Lord."

How do we become great in His eyes? Let's trust the Lord to reveal this to us today.

Preparing to Reflect

"Be still, and know that I am God" (Psalm 46:10). I unwind in my favorite place for prayer and light an Advent candle as a reminder of His presence, warmth, and light. I take a few breaths to still myself right now. Can I open my heart to the loving mystery of God and let Him be who He wants to be for me today?

Prayer

Lord, I desire to give You complete freedom to do whatever You will in my life. Amen.

Story of the Day

"Your wife Elizabeth will bear you a son, and you are to call him John.

He will be a joy and delight to you, and many will rejoice because of his birth, for he will be great in the sight of the Lord. He is never to take wine or other fermented drink, and he will be filled with the Holy Spirit even before he is born. He will bring back many of the people of Israel to the Lord their God. And he will go on before the Lord, in the spirit and power of Elijah, to turn the hearts of the parents to their children and the disobedient to the wisdom of the righteous—to make ready a people prepared for the Lord" (Luke 1:13–17).

Entering the Scene

Have you ever been stunned when the silence breaks? The people of Israel have not heard from God since the time of Malachi, a period of roughly four hundred years. Suddenly, the seams of heaven burst open with hope through Gabriel's words to Zechariah.

Zechariah has never heard from God in such a way! It is unbelievable, almost preposterous, and definitely out of the ordinary. What he hears is unreal, fantasy-like.

How do you see him reacting to the angel's presence and words? Is he questioning himself, "Am I truly seeing what I am seeing?" Can this priest trust what he is hearing? Not only does the angel promise a son, he says this one would be the greatest man who ever lived. "Truly I tell you, among those born of women there has not risen anyone greater than John the Baptist" (Matthew 11:11). The cornucopia of Zechariah's life is overflowing.

What has been your most touching and surprising encounter with God?

Going Deeper

Zechariah learns quickly that no gift given to us is ever solely personal. Wouldn't it be tempting for him to hold on tightly to something that is very precious or call it his own, especially after decades of waiting?

Kahlil Gibran's wisdom reflects the angel's words:

"Your children are not your children. . . .
They come through you but not from you,
And though they are with you yet they belong not to you."

[*The Prophet*]

God gives John not only to Zechariah and Elizabeth, but also to all people. John will bring great joy to their hearts, speak the truth to them like Elijah did, and encourage generational reconciliation. Which of your personal gifts does God want you to share with others?

John's name means "God is gracious," pointing to the reality that one cannot become great unless the Lord is gracious.

The Lord sets John apart for Himself by filling him with the Holy Spirit from conception. Isn't this a wonderful prayer to lift up for the children of all pregnant women?

The Holy Spirit shapes the entirety of John's person from the very beginning. Since the Spirit always works to bring glory to Jesus, He forms John into a very humble yet intense person whose entire existence is centered on Jesus and on preparing a way for Him.

John's heart is not divided, twisted, or bent with multitudes of desires. Instead he is a straight arrow aimed at Jesus' glory. He stands as one of the most focused men in history with a singular intention of his spirit. John's devoted life is the needle that points toward the One True North. John is great because he represents the Greatest!

Which spiritual desire does John's story elicit in you? How single-hearted are you in pursuit of this desire?

Prayer for the Journey

Lord, there is nothing more precious than to be great in Your sight. Shape my life and heart to be truly pleasing to You. Amen.

Your Response

How would you like Jesus to help you to lift Him up this Advent season? Express your desires in writing to Him.

With many blessings,
Liena and Jacqueline

Do You Need a Sign?

Hello again,

In today's reading Zechariah's story keeps unfolding. How will Zechariah respond to this mind-blowing prophecy? How would you respond?

Most of us, like Zechariah, desire to please God and want to believe Him when He speaks something new into our lives. However, we want to be certain that we have heard correctly.

So we ask God for a sign. Yet it is in these moments that God wants us to stretch our faith and take Him at His word. Hebrews 11:6 reminds us: "And without faith it is impossible to please God, because anyone who comes to him must believe that he exists and that he rewards those who earnestly seek him."

Let's dive into today's story and explore faith with Zechariah.

Preparing to Reflect

As I am about to pray, I might make a cup of tea for myself to relax and become calm. With each sip of tea I take, I contemplate God's generosity. He gives His time, attention, and Himself to me.

Can I extend my generosity toward Him by opening my being and inviting Him to spend this time with me in this fellowship of hearts?

Prayer

Lord, increase the spaciousness of my heart for the amazing vision You have for my life. Amen.

Story of the Day

Zechariah asked the angel, "How can I be sure of this? I am an old man and my wife is well along in years."

The angel said to him, "I am Gabriel. I stand in the presence of God, and I have been sent to speak to you and to tell you this good news. And now you will be silent and not able to speak until the day this happens, because you did not believe my words, which will come true at their appointed time."

Meanwhile, the people were waiting for Zechariah and wondering why he stayed so long in the temple. When he came out, he could not speak to them. They realized he had seen a vision in the temple, for he kept making signs to them but remained unable to speak (Luke 1:18–22).

Entering the Scene

Dumbfounded, Zechariah staggers out of the temple, pale as his linen tunic. Drained of all color, he blends in with the white walls of the temple. His lips are parched, not a word escapes. All he sees are people's perplexed and concerned faces. Place yourself into his shoes. What is it like?

Are people relieved that at least he is alive? Were they worried he had offered incense improperly and incurred the wrath of God? Does he motion with his hand pointing to the heavens? What is he trying to say?

They gather he has seen a vision. Their whispers and questions flood the courts. Something has happened, but what?

Going Deeper

At times we are so caught up with our routines that we need to be shocked out of them to see afresh.

Zechariah knows the drill of the ritual, so to speak, and what to expect. He is so used to offering prayers routinely. God's silence is the norm. No wonder he questions everything when God disrupts his complacency. Do you see a little bit of yourself in Zechariah?

Zechariah asks for proof that this will happen. "How can I be sure of this?" In other words, what will the sign be? He has to be certain. The angel Gabriel and his words are not enough.

Zechariah reminds us of a man who went to see Mother Teresa. He asked her to pray for clarity to see his calling and God's direction.

She replied, "Clarity is the last thing you are clinging to and must let go of."

When the man commented that she always seemed to have the clarity he longed for, she responded through laughter, "What I have always had is trust. So I will pray that you trust God." [Brennan Manning, *Ruthless Trust*]

Is God calling you to trust, but you keep asking for one more sign and then another and yet another?

Ironically, Zechariah's chastisement of muteness becomes the sign—not only an external sign that comes and disappears like a rainbow or manna in the desert, but a lasting sign that becomes part of him and changes his heart. We'll see how in our reading tomorrow.

Prayer for the Journey

My loving God, You see all the underlying fears and hesitations preventing me from stepping out in faith. Lead me in such a way that I can say a free, excited, and brave yes to Your kind intentions for my life. Amen.

Your Response
Where do you feel a challenge and hear an invitation in today's reading? Talk to the Lord about your feelings.

Peace to you,
Jacqueline and Liena

Transformed in the Stillness

Dear Friend,

Have you ever spent twenty-four hours in relative quiet and seclusion? What was the outcome of this time for you? We often seek new experiences and new people, thinking these encounters will lead to deep transformations in our lives. But is this always true?

In today's reading, the quiet is God's vehicle for change in Elizabeth and Zechariah. Let their transformation inspire you.

Preparing to Reflect

"The LORD said, 'Go out and stand on the mountain in the presence of the LORD, for the LORD is about to pass by.' Then a great and powerful wind tore the mountains apart and shattered the rocks before the LORD, but the LORD was not in the wind. After the wind there was an earthquake, but the LORD was not in the earthquake. After the earthquake came a fire, but the LORD was not in the fire. And after the fire came a gentle whisper" (1 Kings 19:11–12).

Since God is still speaking, can I do my part of becoming attentive to His Spirit? I gently set my concerns aside and surrender myself to Him. I become curious about His Word for me today.

Prayer

Lord, here I am, waiting and listening for what You have to say. Amen.

Story of the Day

When his time of service was completed, he returned home. After this his wife Elizabeth became pregnant and for five months remained in seclusion. "The Lord has done this for me," she said. "In these days he has shown his favor and taken away my disgrace among the people" (Luke 1:23–25).

Entering the Scene

Finally, the week-long service time at the temple is over. Zechariah is headed home. Who could bear the awkward silence and the question-filled glances any longer?

It is good to be home in the hill country with his beloved wife Elizabeth. The air is fresh and gives him some space. How do you see Zechariah in his surroundings?

Elizabeth does not know anything, but she seems to understand him in that quiet and visceral way.

There is a curious fire burning in her aged eyes. She is luminous with intuitive hope. They dare to embrace each other once again as in the days of their youth, and with God in between them, a child is conceived in a great silence.

The couple is changed beyond words. Have you quietly sat in the darkness waiting for the first light of dawn? Likewise, Elizabeth and Zechariah are watching the dawning miracle of their lives.

Elizabeth becomes heavier with each passing day, but her heart grows lighter. God is slowly and surely peeling away all her shame collected over the years. And Zechariah's faith and recognition of God's greatness grow alongside a baby in his wife's womb. Can you hear God speaking over him: "In repentance and rest is your salvation, in quietness and trust is your strength" (Isaiah 30:15)?

Elizabeth does not leave the house or accept any visitors. She saves it all for a later display of glory.

Going Deeper

Elizabeth's five months of seclusion allow her to taste and savor the goodness and favor of God. The quiet is so abundant with God's presence. She follows the great wisdom: "Be silent before all great things. Let them grow inside you." [Baron Friedrich von Hügel, *Letters to a Niece*] Every grace of God deserves to be marveled at, unwrapped, and savored.

She models for us what a true spiritual retreat is: a time of waiting, watching, and being changed.

She becomes a prophetess while in her seclusion. Later when Elizabeth welcomes Mary, her prophetic words of wisdom spring forth, "Blessed are you among women, and blessed is the child you will bear!" (Luke 1:42).

What are your most significant experiences of God's grace while spending time in solitude with Him?

Upon entering society, Elizabeth's glory is unveiled. Her entire being shines with victorious light for God has taken her disgrace away. All public and internal words of blame and judgment are silenced.

What disgrace and shame has God freed you from in your life? How has this affected others around you? If there is still shame that binds you, we invite you to offer it to God right now. He desires to free and restore you. Ask Him to birth something new in you as He did in Elizabeth.

Prayer for the Journey

My loving God, I thank You for Your passion to free me and take my disgrace away. Lead me to places of quiet and rest. Still me and change me. Amen.

Your Response

What surprises you about Elizabeth's seclusion? What is your response to God's work of taking her disgrace away? Pray and journal your observations from this time of prayer.

Grace and peace,
Your friends

Your Body, His Sanctuary

God's Beloved,

What is your relationship with your physical body? Many of us might answer that this relationship is complicated, filled with varying amounts of love and animosity. But can God actually use our bodies for His greater purposes? In today's devotional, let's see how God answers that question with a resounding yes!

Preparing to Reflect

In the stillness of the space that surrounds me, I close my eyes, relax my body, and invoke the Holy Spirit. In faith I turn my eyes to the Lord. His gaze is gentle, warm, and overflowing with great affection. I let His gaze rest upon me and enfold me in His peace.

Prayer

My loving God, I pray that I can withstand Your fond gaze upon me and not turn away in embarrassment or diminished self-worth. Melt my heart as the sunrays do the most hardened ice. I am here, standing in the sunshine of Your countenance. Help me to receive Your love. Amen.

Story of the Day

In the sixth month of Elizabeth's pregnancy, God sent the angel Gabriel to Nazareth, a town in Galilee, to a virgin pledged to be married to a man named Joseph, a descendant of David. The virgin's name was Mary. The angel went to her and said, "Greetings, you who are highly favored! The Lord is with you."

Mary was greatly troubled at his words and wondered what kind of greeting this might be. But the angel said to her, "Do not be afraid, Mary; you have found favor with God. You will conceive and give birth to a son, and you are to call him Jesus. He will be great and will be called the Son of the Most High. The Lord God will give him the throne of his father David, and he will reign over Jacob's descendants forever; his kingdom will never end" (Luke 1:26–33).

Entering the Scene

The drama of salvation keeps unfolding with thrilling force. Once again, God summons Gabriel into His presence. "What will the next task be?" the angel might wonder.

His Master dispatches him to an insignificant village in Galilee to deliver the most significant message of all times.

Despite the angel's best-chosen words, he startles the virgin girl with a greeting, which in Greek means *rejoice*. Rejoice? Mary is terrified and overwhelmed by this angelic being. Wouldn't we all be a little rattled? A myriad of questions would flow through our minds: "Why me? What does he want? Am I deserving of his visit?"

Has Gabriel thought of how to approach Mary? Perhaps he bends his knee, takes her hand in his, and extends a divine proposal of union with God. His words hold authority and directness, enveloped in even more gentleness, assurance, and affection.

Going Deeper

What an announcement: you are highly favored and you will give birth to the Son of the Most High! How do you receive this lofty calling when you come from such humble means? Perhaps you can relate to Mary.

Gabriel greets Mary as God sees her from heaven: highly favored and worthy of His presence. How are you seen in heaven? Do you find yourself embracing God's announcement of favor upon your life or keeping it at a distance? Gabriel's words unsettle Mary. Yet she does not protest or remind him of her inadequacy.

It is very clear that age, education, and status are not God's main considerations in extending His call. The Father proposes to Mary for He finds a heart and womb just right for His Son's dwelling. He invites her into a full partnership and union of love with Him for the sake of redemption for all.

Reflect on your life for a moment. How do you see God working through your physical self to bring Him glory in this world? How has He done that already? Is it the way you smile, your physical strength, voice, touch, sexuality, or is it simply the way you look at others?

Mary's story with God marks the moment in history of God's ultimate intimacy with a human being. It places our bodies in a position of honor. Jesus' conception, growth in Mary's womb, and birth establish the model of intimacy that God desires in His relationship with us.

I, Liena, will never forget a time of prayer where God whispered to me that we believers are like Mary. I questioned Him as to how this was so. The answer came: "You are pregnant with the Holy Spirit." St. Paul's words rang in my heart, "Don't you know that you yourselves are God's temple and that God's Spirit dwells in your midst?" (1 Corinthians 3:16).

How mindful are you of your "pregnancy" with the Holy Spirit? Who or what are you bringing forth in the newness of life? What difference does this make in your life and in the lives of those around you?

Prayer for the Journey
Loving Father, thank You for creating my body to be the vessel of Your glory. Help me to grow into and carry out my high calling. Amen.

Your Response
Where does today's Scripture take you in your heart? Reveal yourself to the Lord as you pray and journal.

Your sisters in Christ,
Jacqueline and Liena

Will You Say Yes?

Dear Friend,

Yes is such a short word, but the journey toward inner consent can be long, requiring strength and courage. How does Mary arrive at her swift yes to God? Come and draw from the well of her heart and be encouraged toward your own yes.

Preparing to Reflect

"You have searched me, LORD, and you know me. . . . you perceive my thoughts from afar" (Psalm 139:1–2). I am understood and loved; I can just be. I loosen my shoulders and any other tense parts in my body. I let go of any urge to explain myself. I simply let myself rest for a couple of minutes in the presence of a loving and understanding God. Because He knows me deeply, He can lead me precisely to the destination of my journey. I give thanks for this gift.

Prayer

God of all grace, I thank You that Your arms are always open to me. "Search me, God, and know my heart; test me and know my anxious thoughts . . . and lead me in the way everlasting" (Psalm 139:23–24). Amen.

Story of the Day

"How will this be," Mary asked the angel, "since I am a virgin?"

The angel answered, "The Holy Spirit will come on you, and the power of the Most High will overshadow you. So the holy one to be born will be called the Son of God. Even Elizabeth your relative is going to have a child in her old age, and she who was said to be unable to conceive is in her sixth month. For no word from God will ever fail."

"I am the Lord's servant," Mary answered. "May your word to me be fulfilled." Then the angel left her (Luke 1:34–38).

Entering the Scene

Her tiny body shivers and a single question flutters like a bird, "How will this be since I am a virgin?" The answer is so unexpected. She will be the bride of God. The Holy Spirit is going to be the maker of her child. Mary's thoughts take off like a kite. Soar with her for a while.

A single string, the familiar name Elizabeth, pulls Mary's thoughts back. She is not the only one on the road of miracles. Her relative's life, too, has changed forever. How comforting to have a companion into the unknown.

Gabriel stays with Mary until her heart speaks a brave and humble yes to God.

Does Mary sit there for a while and wonder what is next to come? The Holy Spirit is about to overshadow her. What is that moment like when He becomes soul-searingly intimate with her? Savor this mystery.

Going Deeper

What is so remarkable about Mary? She is still a child, most likely between twelve and fourteen years of age, but she sends heaven into ecstatic joy by saying yes to God's proposal. Is that why Jesus praises the faith of a child and calls us to childlike faith? Adulthood lures us into very settled captivities. "Most people, unless the invitation comes to them in early childhood, have already thrust down fierce roots into the heavy clay of the world. Their hands are already gripping hard onto self-interest. They are already partly paralyzed by fear." [Caryll Houselander, *The Reed of God: A New Edition of a Spiritual Classic*]

Mary is still free and brave to say yes to God's outlandish plan. The young virgin asks how this miracle will take place, but she does not doubt that it can happen. She pauses only to bid welcome to her call.

Her heart is wide and open. Mary sees herself no more or less than a vessel of God. Her spirit holds keys to courageous humility.

Can you remember those moments in your life when you knew beyond all knowing that God was directing you and it was only right to proceed despite any fear you might have felt? Only God's glorious presence can bring us to a place of such solid conviction that we can say along with Mary: "I recognize and claim what is happening to me is the will of God."

It is so encouraging to see that God's provision follows Mary's consent. She says yes and the Father provides for the rest. He takes care of Joseph's heart; He makes sure she gets married and not stoned; and He gives a strong and affirmative female companion, Elizabeth, for her journey.

Can you trust in God's loving provision for you? Are there still pending answers to the Lord's invitations in your life today?

Prayer for the Journey

"Take Lord, and receive all my liberty, my memory, my understanding, and my entire will, all that I have and possess. Thou hast given all to me. To Thee, O Lord, I return it. All is Thine, dispose of it wholly according to Thy will. Give me Thy love and Thy grace, for this is sufficient for me" (St. Ignatius of Loyola). Amen.

Your Response
What is your response to the text and letter above? Where in your life do you desire to say yes to God? Journal your thoughts and prayers.

May the Lord bless you and keep you,
Liena and Jacqueline

The Second Week of Advent

The Double Joy

Dear Fellow Traveler,

Do you have a close friend? You enjoy being in each other's company. Your times together are filled with laughter and sharing hearts. Perhaps you have held each other up when life was too heavy to hold alone.

Today let's take a peek into the relationship between Mary and Elizabeth. How does God uniquely craft and grow their friendship?

Preparing to Reflect

God is waiting for me, has time for me, and delights in being with me. I take a few moments to center myself in His presence. I continue by playing or singing a favorite Advent hymn or a worship song to ready my heart for prayer.

Prayer

Father, I come to You now in stillness and with expectancy. I long to know You more. Penetrate every corner of my heart. Reveal to me Your longings for me as I express my longings to You. Amen.

Story of the Day

At that time Mary got ready and hurried to a town in the hill country of Judea, where she entered Zechariah's home and greeted Elizabeth. When Elizabeth heard Mary's greeting, the baby leaped in her womb, and Elizabeth was filled with the Holy Spirit (Luke 1:39–41).

Entering the Scene

Gabriel comes and vanishes as suddenly as a summer storm. Mary is stunned but eager to unwrap the gift of her new life. The Lord is doing something new and amazing in and through her.

Who can she talk to? Who in her family would accept her incredible but odd news? Oh wait, the angel just gave her the clue. Elizabeth would understand her. She would fathom the Lord's work. They both are growing something that is nothing short of miraculous.

Not only that, Mary wants to take part in Elizabeth's joy. She hurries without delay to the hill country of Judea where Zechariah and Elizabeth live. Does she walk or join the caravans on the way? What is this five to eight day, unplanned pilgrimage like? Mary is graced with time and space for the miracle to nestle into her heart and body.

Both Mary and the Holy Spirit greet the expectant Elizabeth in one voice. John, in his mother's womb, recognizes the presence of his Savior and leaps for joy! Jubilation bursts in all of their hearts.

There also is a holy triangular connection between Jesus, John, and the Holy Spirit. It is astonishing how there is a recognition of each other in the spiritual realm.

John does not meet Jesus for the first time in the river of Jordan at Jesus' baptism. In humility, Jesus comes to Elizabeth and John in Mary's womb. Right from the start He is a servant and the One who initiates a relationship. Take a moment to contemplate God's humility in your own life.

A holy dance erupts between John, Jesus, Mary, Elizabeth, and the Holy Spirit in a circle of joy. The Holy Spirit threads them all together. Where in your life do you experience a bond of the Holy Spirit?

Going Deeper

In this passage, we feel an electrifying, intimate, and triangular connection between Mary, Elizabeth, and the Holy Spirit.

The presence of the Lord growing in Mary confirms within Elizabeth the miracle that God is performing in her own body. She can't contain it; she has to shout! Elizabeth's exclamation, prompted by the Holy Spirit, confirms in Mary what the Lord is doing in her. There can be no mistaking that God is present in His loving grace.

He leaves neither of them alone but gives them to each other to walk out this journey of faith, to share joy, and to alleviate shame. These two women's souls are brought together for a common mission in this world. They don't have to do it on their own but in the company of each other's assurance, confirmation, understanding, and support.

Only He could come up with the idea to unite two women at such opposite ends of the spectrum: a woman well past her childbearing prime and a virgin girl heralding a new era for all humanity.

Jacqueline and I have been blessed to share a similar connection. We call out each other's essence through encouragement and loving confrontation. We feel refreshed and renewed in each other's company. An abundance of shared grace covers each of our shortcomings. We have cried with and encouraged each other through a long-distance relationship, unmet longings, broken relationships, failing out of medical school, and cancer. And now we share the common call to write. We are searching for God together and finding each other in a much deeper way than ever before.

What people have God placed in your life to share a common faith and journey? If this is your deep desire, but it has not happened yet, take a moment to express your yearning to the Lord.

Prayer for the Journey

Thank You for the gift of each friend who accompanies me on this walk of faith and calls me into deeper relationship with You. Amen.

Your Response

What are your deepest longings for friendship? Do you desire for the Holy Spirit to weave His presence into your relationships? Bring these requests to God in prayer.

With blessing,
Your Advent friends

Inherit a Blessing!

Dear Friend,

So many times the Scriptures invite us to express the joy of the Lord with the entirety of our strength. "Sing, Daughter Zion; shout aloud, Israel! Be glad and rejoice with all your heart, Daughter Jerusalem!" (Zephaniah 3:14). But how many times have you actually witnessed someone expressing joy to this extent? Today you are about to. Let it spread to your heart!

Preparing to Reflect

"Holy, holy, holy is the LORD Almighty; the whole earth is full of his glory" (Isaiah 6:3). What does this mean for me as I am about to pray? I take a few deep breaths as I appreciate God's all pervasive glory around and within me.

Prayer

Lord, make me fully alive to Your presence. Amen.

Story of the Day

In a loud voice she exclaimed: "Blessed are you among women, and blessed is the child you will bear! But why am I so favored, that the mother of my

Lord should come to me? Blessed is she who has believed that the Lord would fulfill his promises to her!"

Mary stayed with Elizabeth for about three months and then returned home (Luke 1:42–43, 45, 56).

Entering the Scene

Elizabeth meets Mary and embraces her with a loud squeal of joy! Without any means of external communication, Elizabeth sees through to the unfolding miracle in her cousin's life. If you were Elizabeth, what would be happening in you right now?

Mary shares Elizabeth's last trimester. How do you see them spending time together? How do you see them savoring and celebrating God's goodness day after day surrounded by the beauty of the countryside?

We see their hands stroking each other bellies with praises and laughter rising to the heavens. Sharing meals, preparing for John's arrival, and taking walks mark the rhythm of their days.

How is Zechariah observing this double growing miracle right in front of his eyes? Place yourself in his position and watch with him. What do you see?

Going Deeper

Elizabeth is so taken by Mary's visit that she says, "Why am I so favored, that the mother of my Lord should come to me?" This passage reminds us of King David in 2 Samuel 6:9 who exclaims, "How can the ark of the LORD ever come to me?" The ark of the covenant was the sacred place of the Most High, the dwelling place of God. Mary is like the ark who carries Jesus, the King of the Universe, wherever she goes.

Upon Mary's entry into Zechariah's home, blessing upon blessing like streams of living water gush from Elizabeth's heart.

What does it mean to bless someone? The word used in this text is *eulogeo*, which in Greek means to "speak well of" and "praise someone." This is where the English word *eulogy* comes from: "an honoring tribute to the departed." But how about blessing the living as Elizabeth does?

Have you ever experienced someone delivering words of blessing to you in such a way that your heart expanded? It is like you are given new wings to fly! That is what Elizabeth is doing in Mary's life. Blessing is always prophetic because it calls forward a person's true identity and speaks of hope and the future.

Elizabeth's blessing is four-fold. She blesses and confirms Mary's faith for believing God will carry out His promises to her. She also honors Mary by naming her new identity of being the mother of God. Elizabeth declares a new era in Mary's life. Mary is no longer an invisible peasant girl but a new rising star among all women. Lastly, Elizabeth extols the fruit of her womb, Jesus.

We all are called to intentionally speak well of all people so that we might also inherit a blessing (1 Peter 3:9). How do you practice this in your life?

Prayer for the Journey

Lord, I desire to name and honor the true heart of others. You call me to bless and inherit the blessing. Help me to enter into the full circle of blessings. Amen.

Your Response

What has moved you in today's reading? Talk to the Lord about it. What do you sense Him saying to you?

May the Lord keep you,
Your sisters in Christ

Mindfulness of God

Our Advent Friend,

What is your usual response when people praise and acknowledge you? Today we will witness Mary's reply to Elizabeth's words of blessing. She does not dismiss or shy away from them. Instead she confidently bursts into a glorious song of praise to the living God because of them. Allow her exuberance to inspire you!

Preparing to Reflect

"For in him we live and move and have our being" (Acts 17:28). I am inseparable from my loving God. Can I close my eyes and envision myself being a fish in the ocean of God's presence? I let myself feel the immense freedom and joy of swimming in Him and with Him without limits.

Prayer

"Praise the LORD, my soul; all my inmost being, praise his holy name" (Psalm 103:1). My loving God, I thank You that I am in You and You are in me. I am ready to receive all You want to grant me in this time of prayer. Amen.

Story of the Day

And Mary said: "My soul glorifies the Lord and my spirit rejoices in God my Savior, for he has been mindful of the humble state of his servant. From now on all generations will call me blessed, for the Mighty One has done great things for me—holy is his name" (Luke 1:46–49).

Entering the Scene

Have you tried to start a fire just from one piece of wood? We all know it does not work well. As wood ignites wood, so do we as human beings ignite the spark within each other.

The spark from Elizabeth's soul springs to Mary's heart by way of the Holy Spirit. Elizabeth's words of blessing ignite Mary's inner flame; she breaks out in passionate, prophetic praise.

Notice how her entire being is involved in magnifying the living God: her voice, her spirit, and her soul. "My soul magnifies the Lord, and my spirit rejoices in God my Savior."

Can you recall a similar event in your life when someone deeply understood and validated your spiritual experience that led to joyful response and action?

Imagine standing there next to the first two prophetesses of the New Testament. What is the body posture of these two women? What else do you sense and notice? How do you get involved in their joy?

Going Deeper

Heaven crashes into earth. Mary's life has changed already, "For He has looked upon the low station and humiliation of His handmaiden" (Luke 1:48 AMP) and has exalted her above all women.

Mary's story holds such an amazing hope for all who are unseen and unheard. She is a mentor and patroness of all people who experience insignificance in this world. Mary's message to the abused, the neglected, and the oppressed is clear: "God is on your side. He can and wants to change your reality by bringing you out of the shadows of life into His wonderful light. Believe!" Has this been true in your life? If not, do you believe that it is God's desire for you?

Mary strikes us as a person of grounded humility who frankly acknowledges her insignificance but does not allow that to define her in a finite way, hold her back, or hinder God's work. She is able to take her ego out of the equation and let God freely move in her and through her. She is so humble, yet courageous—the perfect combination for God's kingdom work.

Prayer for the Journey

Lord, You raised Mary up and yet kept her heart humble. May the fruit of my liberation lead me into joyous exclamation: "He has done great things for me. Holy is His name!"

Your Response

What amazes and inspires you about Mary? How would you like to resemble her? Journal your impressions. Pray your thoughts.

In prayer for you,
Liena and Jacqueline

God's Revolution

God's Friend,

Have the events of these days ever left you longing for justice? So much in our world can seem out of order. We may even shout at times, "God, where are You in the midst of this mess?"

In the story that we will read today, Mary assures us that our God loves justice and is the champion of those who suffer in any way. Let's discover how He will right the wrongs of our world.

Preparing to Reflect

"Because he turned his ear to me, I will call on him as long as I live" (Psalm 116:2) I light my Advent candle and connect with the stillness and beauty of the flickering light. I close my eyes and behold the image of God listening intently to me and wanting to serve me now. How does this make me feel? Can I become quiet and respond to Him in the same way?

Prayer

Lord Jesus, You reign over the universe, yet You serve us with the towel wrapped around Your waist. I still myself now and consent to Your work in my life and the world around me. Amen.

Story of the Day

"His mercy extends to those who fear him, from generation to generation. He has performed mighty deeds with his arm; he has scattered those who are proud in their inmost thoughts. He has brought down rulers from their thrones but has lifted up the humble. He has filled the hungry with good things but has sent the rich away empty. He has helped his servant Israel, remembering to be merciful to Abraham and his descendants forever, just as he promised our ancestors" (Luke 1:50–55).

Entering the Scene

Can one restrain a flowing stream? Of course you can't. Mary is a prophet who shouts from the "rooftops" in a loud, convincing, and exuberant voice. Mary's song is unrelenting.

The Master Weaver has entwined Mary's life into the tapestry of all future generations. A lowly young girl becomes a landmark for the beginning of a new kingdom where the humble are raised up and the hungry are satisfied. It is the advent of God's revolution for all humankind.

How would you feel if you heard this message? Frightened, surprised, startled, or maybe overjoyed?

Going Deeper

What is the heart of Mary's message? She proclaims to the entire world—including John the Baptist—that things are about to change dramatically. She announces the coming of a new kingdom, a new order. The world, as people have known it, is about to change.

Big surprises are on the way: the humble and the hungry will be satisfied. They will rise to the top in this new kingdom whereby the proud and the rich will be frustrated and their worldly acclaims will be of no importance. Think for a moment, why do we love stories of an underdog's triumph? Do we recognize the workings of God's kingdom in them?

Mary's words make everyone rethink their standing. Her prophecy calls for an adjustment of every single heart, a complete change of perspective. Mary's words are a prelude to her Son's message years later:

> "Blessed are the poor in spirit,
>> for theirs is the kingdom of heaven.
> Blessed are those who mourn, for they will be comforted.
> Blessed are the meek, for they will inherit the earth.
> Blessed are those who hunger and thirst for righteousness,
>> for they will be filled.
> Blessed are the merciful, for they will be shown mercy.
> Blessed are the pure in heart, for they will see God.
> Blessed are the peacemakers,
>> for they will be called children of God.
> Blessed are those who are persecuted because of righteousness,
>> for theirs is the kingdom of heaven.
> Blessed are you when people insult you, persecute you and falsely say all kinds of evil against you because of me. Rejoice and be glad, because great is your reward in heaven, for in the same way they persecuted the prophets who were before you" (Matthew 5:3–12).

How much are you aware of God's kingdom values? Have you seen His kingdom principles at work in your life?

Mary's song of praise ends on a note of God's faithfulness to all Abraham's descendants, the people of faith. Because of her Son, you are one of those people of faith.

Prayer for the Journey
Yes, Lord, may Your Kingdom come and Your will be done on the earth as it is displayed in heaven. Amen.

Your Response
In what areas of your life would you like to see God's revolution? Journal your thoughts.

His children,
Jacqueline and Liena

_____

_____

_____

_____

_____

_____

_____

_____

_____

_____

_____

_____

_____

_____

_____

_____

_____

_____

_____

_____

_____

_____

_____

_____

A New Day!

Dear Advent Pilgrim,

The miracle of birth never ceases to astound us. Have you ever witnessed someone's birth? If you haven't, you are about to. If you have, we invite you into this wonder once again. Elizabeth is about to deliver her son. Are you ready?

Preparing to Reflect

"For with you is the fountain of life; in your light we see light" (Psalm 36:9). There is no new life without light. In the silence of this moment, I become mindful of all the light around me and in me. I give thanks for this gift and become aware of the new things sprouting in my life because of it.

Prayer

Lord, I give thanks for the warmth and power of Your light in my life. I bare my darkest places and barrenness to You for Your transformation. Amen.

Story of the Day

When it was time for Elizabeth to have her baby, she gave birth to a son. Her neighbors and relatives heard that the Lord had shown her great mercy, and they shared her joy.

On the eighth day they came to circumcise the child, and they were going to name him after his father Zechariah, but his mother spoke up and said, "No! He is to be called John."

They said to her, "There is no one among your relatives who has that name."

Then they made signs to his father, to find out what he would like to name the child. He asked for a writing tablet, and to everyone's astonishment he wrote, "His name is John." Immediately his mouth was opened and his tongue set free, and he began to speak, praising God. All the neighbors were filled with awe, and throughout the hill country of Judea people were talking about all these things. Everyone who heard this wondered about it, asking, "What then is this child going to be?" For the Lord's hand was with him (Luke 1:57–66).

Entering the Scene

The cry of the aged and laboring woman splits the air. Through joy and pain, finally, a son is born. Streams of gladness wash away the last of her shame and disappointment. It is truly a new day.

Take a wide-angled view of the scene. This moment seems to have it all: relief, tears, laughter, and pulsating delight. Hearts and hands are raised up in effervescent praise.

Elizabeth and Zechariah's personal joy pours over into their community. On the eighth day they gather for John's circumcision. The father should take the leading role in this ceremony. Yet Zechariah is more on the periphery of this event due to his muteness.

The people take charge and want to name the baby after his father. To everybody's surprise, Elizabeth boldly rises to her full stature and proclaims firmly: "No! He is to be called John." Her voice is made confident by God's tangible love and presence in her life.

Confusion and mumbling runs through the crowd. People look at each other in disbelief. "Who in their family is named John? Zechariah's brother? An uncle or grandfather?" The answer is, "No one!"

Distrustful of a woman's voice, they all turn to Zechariah for an answer. Zechariah motions for a writing tablet and scribbles out the words, "His name is John."

His obedience to the Lord unlocks his lips in an instant. After nine months of silence, Zechariah breaks into praise and sends the crowd into wonder. A holy moment.

What have been those moments in your life when you have wanted "to take off your shoes" in the presence of something absolutely astonishing or sacred?

Going Deeper

What is the real issue in the family's dispute over John's name? Conventionalism. It would be right to name the boy after his father indicating that he will walk in his footsteps. Not in this case. John's call is distinctly different from his father' vocation. God calls him within his unique name, reflecting His hope for John's life.

What is your sacred name, felt deeply in your heart, perhaps not known to others? Who are you to become?

Following the guidance of God's Spirit, Elizabeth and Zechariah deviate from the well-trodden path. In their advanced age they display a fascinating internal strength in breaking from the old patterns and orthodox customs. The couple announces God's given name for their son.

Reflect on your life for a moment. How has God challenged you to exchange the usual patterns and behaviors inherited from your family line with different and new ones?

God's involvement in our lives most certainly will bring unanticipated and surprising turns. This often causes initial perplexity and questioning, as we see in today's text. The unexpectedness of God's choices keeps us in a state of suspense and wonder.

Reflect now on the playful, original, and inventive side of God and your openness to His surprises. How do you find yourself? Open? Resistant? Fearful? Do you trust that all His motives are loving?

Prayer for the Journey

Lord, fill my heart with laughter and my lips with shouts of joy as I witness the surprises of life that You bring my way. Amen.

Your Response

What has John's birth story stirred in you? Bring these internal movements to your time of prayer. Write to the Lord.

Advent blessings,
Your sisters in Christ

Zechariah Speaks!

Shalom,

Can you recall a time in your life when you received something significant from the Lord and could not wait to share it with someone?

Zechariah has been silent for months. He has experienced the Lord in significant ways, and his heart is bursting with new revelations. And finally, his lips open like a floodgate. What does he have to say?

Preparing to Reflect
Prayer is listening with my entire being and responding to what I have heard. Am I ready to listen? I prepare my body to be relaxed and at ease. Is my heart receptive and open? With each breath I pray, "Arise, Holy Spirit."

Prayer
"Open my lips, Lord, and my mouth will declare your praise" (Psalm 51:15).

Story of the Day
His father Zechariah was filled with the Holy Spirit and prophesied:

"Praise be to the Lord, the God of Israel,
　　because he has come to his people and redeemed them.
He has raised up a horn of salvation for us
　　in the house of his servant David
(as he said through his holy prophets of long ago),
salvation from our enemies
　　and from the hand of all who hate us—
to show mercy to our ancestors
　　and to remember his holy covenant,
　　the oath he swore to our father Abraham,
to rescue us from the hand of our enemies,
　　and to enable us to serve him without fear
　　in holiness and righteousness
　　　　before him all our days" (Luke 1:67–75).

Entering the Scene

Zechariah speaks! After a little more than nine months of a straining and groaning to communicate, a torrent of words pours out. Is this the wisdom that emerges after a long silence? Is this what happens when the Holy Spirit fills you? If you were there, what would you notice?

The guests can't believe what they are hearing. They are astonished upon hearing sounds from the man who has been mute. Even more, they are amazed by the words themselves: "He has come to his people and redeemed them, . . . He has raised up a horn of salvation . . . , salvation from our enemies and from the hand of all who hate us." Zechariah's community knows the promises that God has made to their ancestors and His faithfulness throughout the generations. Yet, could this moment, this very moment, be the *one*?

Going Deeper

Zechariah paints with very bold strokes the picture of God's pursuit of His people. Without a doubt, the initiative is with God. "He has come to his people, and redeemed them." He is the God who is always coming and reaching out in love. "We pursue God because, and only because, He has first put an urge within us that spurs us to the pursuit." [A.W. Tozer, *The Pursuit of God*]

Take a moment to remember the origins of your own faith journey. How did God draw your attention to Himself? Who did He send to point the way to Him? You might want to offer the gift of appreciation to the One who has loved you first.

And even today, in what ways do you feel God pursuing you? What are your "God sightings" in this season? Maybe you are able to see His presence right away, or perhaps you struggle to recognize it. Be gentle and prayerful as you tap into the perceptiveness and memory of your heart.

God's initiative, salvation, and redemption from the enemy stem from His faithfulness to generations long ago and His unwavering commitment to you and me. God remembers the covenant entered into in, the oath sworn, and promises made to His people. He cannot be or do otherwise. He does not go against His nature no matter how unfaithful humankind has been.

There have been times when I, Liena, have been overwhelmed by the sense of God's consistent forgiveness despite my continual falling. I have called out to Him in disbelief: "Why do You continue to forgive me? Why do You continue to bless me?" The answer always rings clear as a bell: "Because that's who I am. I want My goodness to disarm your resistance so you can be like Me."

This is the exact point that Zechariah is making. God gives His Son and defeats our enemy so we can respond wholeheartedly and "serve him without fear in holiness and righteousness before him all our days."

Prayer for the Journey

Thank You, my dear Promise Keeper, for Your faithfulness to me. Your pursuit of me continues throughout all my risings and fallings. Incite me to respond to Your love bravely, wholeheartedly, and steadily, encouraging my fellow pilgrims along the way. Amen.

Your Response

What stands out to you from today's reading and reflection? What does God want to communicate to you in the quiet during this season of Advent?

Your Advent companions,
Liena and Jacqueline

Midwifing Life

Christ's Beloved,

There is such beauty in being known and such power in being encouraged to live according to the essence of your being. We all need to be called forward in our becoming. Today we will witness a beautifully poignant story of a father prophetically midwifing and blessing his son's core identity. You might recognize yourself in this story.

Preparing to Reflect

"The LORD your God is with you, the Mighty Warrior who saves. He will take great delight in you; in his love he will no longer rebuke you, but will rejoice over you with singing" (Zephaniah 3:17). I take a few deep breaths and place myself in this scene. How do I truly feel about being loved by God in this way? I offer the reality of my heart as I come to this time of prayer.

Prayer

Thank You, Lord, that nothing can hinder Your love toward me. Help me to receive Your words of encouragement for me today. Amen.

Story of the Day

> *"And you, my child, will be called a prophet of the Most High;*
> *for you will go on before the Lord to prepare the way for him,*
> *to give his people the knowledge of salvation*
> *through the forgiveness of their sins,*
> *because of the tender mercy of our God,*
> *by which the rising sun will come to us from heaven*
> *to shine on those living in darkness*
> *and in the shadow of death,*
> *to guide our feet into the path of peace" (Luke 1:76–79).*

Entering the Scene

Zechariah turns to his son. His eyes meet John's with utmost intentionality. Can you see Zechariah cradling John and speaking these words over him? The well-worn lines in his face crinkle into a smile as he speaks of the fulfillment of God's promises. What touches your heart as you picture this scene?

There are people in our lives who convey an unforgettable message with only a look. Can you recall a person whose piercing eyes of love, good wishes, or prophetic words have remained with you over time? I, Liena, remember one of my professors at university who singled me out of the crowd and spoke over me prophetic words of God's kind intentions for my life. Those words have been my constant companion and reminder for over twenty years. They are a guiding light.

Going Deeper

Zechariah addresses John in the most touching and sincere way. "And you, my child, will be called a prophet of the Most High." How gracefully he blesses and calls forward his son's destiny. Zechariah names his son's essence and calling, as he is known in heaven.

In doing so, he invites you and me to be keenly aware and attentive to recognize the essence of our own children and peers and to call it forward through encouragement.

Zechariah demonstrates that effective parenting, mentoring, and friendships involve being prophetically relational. We all need to experience someone hearing from God on our behalf and blessing us with His words of hope and direction. Who in your life has recognized your essence and has encouraged you to pursue your calling in this world? I believe we all still share Adam's prophetic call to name the essence of the one before us.

I remember with tears the day my atheist high school teacher proclaimed: "Liena, you should be a minister." In humility, she was able to put aside her personal beliefs and to simply name what she saw. God used a perceptive unbeliever to change my life's trajectory.

The Advent season invites us to slow down and truly see people at the core of their being. How intentional and committed are you to seeing, naming, and calling people forward in their destiny? Could it be your new and joyous commitment?

Prayer for the Journey

Father, help us to risk seeming foolish or presumptuous if You call us to speak prophetically into someone's life. Help us to receive visionary words spoken over us with wisdom, discernment, and an open heart. Amen.

Your Response
Ponder today's message. Where does it want to take you? Journal and pray.

May the presence of the Lord enfold you,
Liena and Jacqueline

The Third Week of Advent

The Necessity of Preparation

Greetings,

If you were to interview John about his calling, the answer would be short and sweet, "Born to prepare." It's no secret that most people would prefer to be the star rather than the one to prepare the way for someone else to shine.

Ironically, John's ministry turns out to be immensely powerful. "Truly I tell you, among those born of women there has not risen anyone greater than John the Baptist" (Matthew 11:11). Let's see why and how.

Preparing to Reflect

John and Jesus both needed solitude to give their full and undivided attention to the Father. I follow their example. I listen for a moment to my favorite music or the sounds in nature to help me to clear internal space for my communion with God. Once I feel relaxed and focused, I ask the Holy Spirit to accompany me in this time of prayer.

Prayer

Lord, teach me the art of giving myself away to become a part of Your greater glory. Amen.

Story of the Day

The beginning of the good news about Jesus the Messiah, the Son of God, as it is written in Isaiah the prophet: "I will send my messenger ahead of you, who will prepare your way"—"a voice of one calling in the wilderness, 'Prepare the way for the Lord, make straight paths for him'" (Mark 1:1–3).

During the high-priesthood of Annas and Caiaphas, the word of God came to John son of Zechariah in the wilderness (Luke 3:2).

Entering the Scene

Isn't it intriguing that "the beginning of the good news" about Jesus doesn't really begin with Him but with someone else? His cousin John is the short but powerful preface to the incarnation story. Who have been the people God has used to prepare a way for your life and vocation?

Even though John is aware of the need to prepare a way for Jesus, he knows he must wait for the timing to be right. Nonetheless, is John engaged in moments of restless eagerness like all of us at times? "When God? How much longer?"

What is it like for John to finally receive the word from God that the time is ripe? How do you see it coming to him? In a loud voice, a whisper, or an inner knowing? How do you usually hear from God?

After receiving the Word of God, John gives himself fully to this ministry without reservation.

Going Deeper

John lives to prepare the way for Jesus. Does the fact that even Jesus needs someone to help level the ground in people's hearts surprise you in any way? We find it so humbling. It makes us appreciate the notion of preparation on a much deeper level.

No matter how powerful the teacher is and no matter how convincing the message, it still necessitates a readiness and an openness in the recipient's heart. In this way we see Jesus' humility and the Father's wisdom.

Let's reflect for a second. How many sincere attempts, good ideas, creative projects, and even relationships have you witnessed failing because of a lack of preparation? Our impatience and pride pave the road for failure. Preparation is as equally important as culmination.

The ever-increasing pace of modern life can give us an illusion that the end result is more important than preparation. It rushes us through very important stages of increased revelation. The season of Advent teaches us the relevance of preparation.

When Jesus comes, John, the most powerful and passionate man, humbly recedes into the background as if he never existed. "He must increase, but I *must* decrease" (John 3:30 KJV). Are we yielding to the flow of life that calls for letting go, graceful decreasing, or shifting of direction when something or someone greater comes?

Prayer for the Journey

My loving God, You are the Master of timing, the ebb and the flow of life. Give me the wisdom to recognize for whom and what I need to prepare a way. Grant me the discernment of when to live intensely and when to let go. Amen.

Your Response

What is stirred up in you right now? What challenges you? What affirms you? Express your heart to God in journaling and prayer.

Blessings of grace and peace,
Your friends

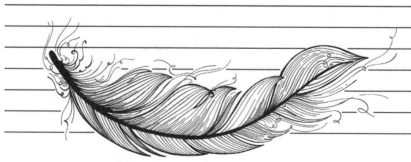

Are You a Person of Integrity and Mercy?

Dear Friend,

Do you ever feel like so much of life happens between the lines? If you conveyed the big-picture brushstrokes of your life to someone, so much of the richness in the details, the grittiness of what really happened, would be lost. Today's passage is like that.

Matthew tells us the story of the birth of Jesus but leaves us hungering to know more of what happened between the lines. His account leaves wide, glorious space in which to imagine the details.

Preparing to Reflect

As I am about to embark on the text of this day, I turn down the volume of my inner noise. I let my eyes linger on a crucifix, an icon, a painting, a candle, or other symbol of God's presence to help me to calm down and ready myself for this time of prayer. I gently put aside all the known facts and approach this story with new eyes and an open heart.

Prayer

Lord, Holy Spirit, speak to me in a fresh way. Bring to life the important messages between the lines. Amen.

Story of the Day

This is how the birth of Jesus the Messiah came about: His mother Mary was pledged to be married to Joseph, but before they came together, she was found to be pregnant through the Holy Spirit. Because Joseph her husband was faithful to the law, and yet did not want to expose her to public disgrace, he had in mind to divorce her quietly (Matthew 1:18–19).

Entering the Scene

If you are married, do you remember the anticipation of your special day? Two hearts fill with excitement and expectation as the wedding approaches.

In the passage of Scripture above, new life is about to dawn, and then the most shocking news emerges. Mary is already pregnant! How does Joseph find that out? Does Mary break the news to him? We can only imagine the intensity of this stressful conversation. Or maybe he overhears two people exchanging the latest bit of juicy gossip. Life drains from Joseph's face, his legs grow weak, and his heart's dreams are washed away in the most powerful shockwave.

Have you ever experienced the deep pain of betrayal? Be Joseph's companion for a minute. Sit with him, and put your arms around him. What is your togetherness like? Are you prompted to say anything to him? Is he saying anything to you? How does Joseph make sense of the astonishing details of his fiancée's pregnancy? Does he chide himself for trusting that Mary would be nothing but faithful to him?

Now, what is Mary experiencing? How do you sense her feelings at this time? Most women in her condition and in that society would have been absolutely terrified. However, we have to remember that she trusts God's promise in the midst of these unbelievable circumstances.

Have you ever experienced peace, consolation, strength, or even joy that transcended all reality, logic, or the madness of life?

Going Deeper

What behaviors would you normally expect from a man who has been deceived? Anger, lashing out, accusation, and vengeance—any or all of these would be quite conceivable.

However, we witness in Joseph a different response all together. He looks beyond his personal hurt and moves in the spirit of righteousness, compassion, and mercy. He proves himself to be a man of deep humility and a sensitive heart. We see how he is a perfect match as a husband for Mary. No wonder God chose him for this mission!

Because of his faith and integrity, Joseph cannot follow through with his original plan and marry Mary for that would indicate his disregard for the sin of adultery. He chooses instead to honor her by quietly severing their engagement, thereby saving Mary from public disgrace and stoning. It affirms the truth that a standard for good relationship is not shaming.

Does this bring up any memories for you of choosing forgiveness over personal retaliation? What have you sacrificed in your life to guard the honor of another person? Has anyone ever done that for you? Take a moment to reflect.

This isn't a decision that Joseph comes to lightly. We can imagine him turning the issue over in his mind, pondering the details from every angle, and struggling to come to a place of peace about what to do. Can you recall moments of deep anguish in your own decision making?

The beauty of it all is that God is present in Joseph's turmoil and closely observes his discernment journey. God does not rescue Joseph right away. He lets Joseph wrestle, grow, and emerge out of his struggle as a more mature man. What can we learn from this? Can you trust God's timing for yourself?

As soon as Joseph makes his decision on the basis of integrity and mercy, God honors him by sending an angel in his dream. What is to come for him?

Prayer for the Journey

Steady me, O Lord, in Your promises and give me Your peace and consolation that transcend all of life's storms. Help me to stand in integrity and move with mercy. Amen.

Your Response

What is your heart's response to Joseph's and Mary's journey? How do you relate to them? What is your heart reading between the lines? Journal, if you so desire.

May the Lord bless you,
Liena and Jacqueline

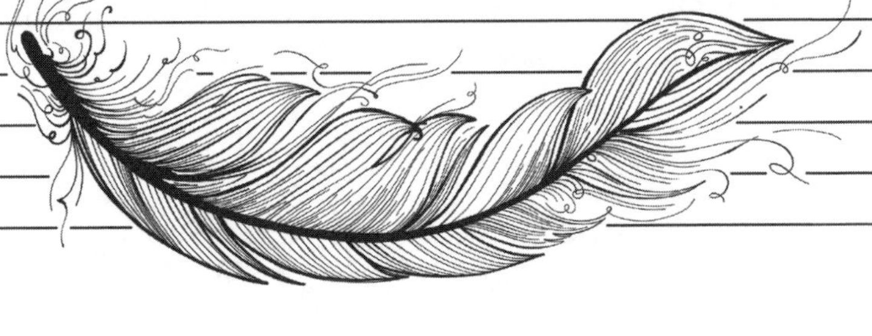

Are You Listening to Your Dreams?

Beloved Pilgrim,

Today's reading starts with the word *but*. Does it remind you of any situations in your own life? Your decision process may have looked like this: you have struggled like Joseph, thinking you have heard from the Lord. You have made up your mind, so now you can move on. Then God intervenes and changes everything.

How has God intervened in your life and changed its course completely after you have made a decision?

We invite you to stay with Joseph and see what happens next in his life and also in your own heart.

Preparing to Reflect

God is so generous in offering Himself and His Word to me. I take a moment to examine my own generosity toward Him. I have the opportunity to offer my time and attention to Him right now. I place my hands on my knees, palms up, as a way of saying, "Here I am, Lord. I am ready to give and to receive."

Prayer

God of true generosity, I pray that today I can freely welcome Your Word in my heart. Amen.

Story of the Day

But after he had considered this, an angel of the Lord appeared to him in a dream and said, "Joseph son of David, do not be afraid to take Mary home as your wife, because what is conceived in her is from the Holy Spirit. She will give birth to a son, and you are to give him the name Jesus, because he will save his people from their sins."

All this took place to fulfill what the Lord had said through the prophet: "The virgin will conceive and give birth to a son, and they will call him Immanuel" (which means "God with us").

When Joseph woke up, he did what the angel of the Lord had commanded him and took Mary home as his wife. But he did not consummate their marriage until she gave birth to a son. And he gave him the name Jesus (Matthew 1:20–25).

Entering the Scene

And then there is the dream, a visiting angel in the night. He gets in through the back door of Joseph's soul. The dream is supremely more real than anything reason or rationale can offer.

The directives given to Joseph are so plain: marry Mary and name the child "Jesus." God demonstrates His own tender heart toward Joseph by giving him details and filling in the gaping spaces. He explains the circumstances of Mary's pregnancy and then instructs him on how to proceed.

Can you imagine Joseph's astonishment at this announcement and his great relief in knowing that Mary has not been with another man? Can you relate this to events in your own life when one piece of clarifying information changed your entire perspective and direction?

What does it mean to this man to wake up and realize that God has chosen him to raise His Son? Does he think himself worthy of this great calling?

What is their reunion like when Joseph comes to Mary and says, "I know. I had a dream, and God told me everything."

True to his nature, Joseph's immediate response to the dream is obedience. He marries her. Showing his great honor for Mary and for the Lord, he denies himself physically until the birth of Jesus. When the time comes, he obeys his second directive and gives this child the name "Jesus."

Going Deeper

Both the Old and New Testaments reveal many accounts of God speaking to people through dreams. Joseph receives guidance in this way, not once but twice. Is it because God knows that Joseph believes in this truth deeply and is sensitive to it?

His dream is so convincing and impactful that upon waking he is transformed and empowered to change his direction completely. This mystical and, at the same time, concrete experience guides him and motivates him instantly to move forward. What is your relationship with your dreams? Are you open to hearing God's guidance while you sleep?

I, Liena, have been guided to pray for people through dreams sensing impending danger. There also have been dreams that have blatantly revealed the truth about my inmost state and called for a change. Some have indicated the future. In one of my most beautiful dreams I experienced God's gaze upon me. I woke up a changed person. Like Joseph I was filled with the immensity of God's love for me and comforted by His stark-naked knowledge of me. I still hold onto that "in-love" gaze.

Dreams are autonomous. They are like another personality in us. They have a life of their own. Amazing. . . . Dreams tell it like it is. They don't sugar coat things. They alert us when we are going down the wrong road or are in danger. They also give us hope and clues as to how to get back on the right road. [Robert, L. Haden, Jr., *Unopened Letters from God: Using Biblical Dreams to Unlock Nightly Dreams*]

What Joseph hears and sees in his dream is amazing, overwhelming, and requires action. Only a few can withstand the glorious weight of God's call.

Are we listening not only to our dreams as we sleep but also to the other kind of dreams, the ones deeply imbedded in our being?

Prayer for the Journey

Lord, watch over my heart during the watches of the night. Use my rest and non-resistance to speak tenderly and convincingly to me. Amen.

Your Response

What have been some of your more significant dreams lately? Have you written them down? Have you unpacked them, prayed over them, and explored them? Take some time to start this journey today.

With love,
Your fellow pilgrims

Finding Hidden Grace

Good Day,

Thank you for faithfully continuing this Advent journey with us. Today we are joining Joseph and Mary as they make their way from Nazareth to Bethlehem. On this crowded road, they walk under the heavy yoke of Roman oppression with their fellow Israelites. We invite you to walk with them.

Preparing to Reflect

I am here to rest with the Lord and take a walk with Him in this Scripture scene. I still myself and become aware of the burdens I carry this Advent season. What do I need to lie down? I am freed as I place my burdens at Jesus' feet. I take His extended hand to walk on the road leading to new discoveries.

Prayer

Lord, I cast my cares on You for You free me and sustain me. Amen.

Story of the Day:

In those days Caesar Augustus issued a decree that a census should be taken of the entire Roman world. (This was the first census that took place while

Quirinius was governor of Syria.) And everyone went to their own town to register.

So Joseph also went up from the town of Nazareth in Galilee to Judea, to Bethlehem the town of David, because he belonged to the house and line of David. He went there to register with Mary, who was pledged to be married to him and was expecting a child (Luke 2:1–5).

Entering the Scene

We hear the rumble of horses' hooves against the hard ground and see the clouds of dust arising. We hear the voices of messengers reading out loud the decree of compulsory registration. The crowd flashes angry looks at the emissaries and murmurs words full of hatred. Yes, this is one more reminder that the Roman enemy rules. Every drop of Israel's dignity is wrung out. Surely the census is taken to increase tax revenues!

Joseph hears this directive with a heavy heart. How will they make this journey that is eight to ten days long? Mary is so close to delivering their child. Imagine yourself in Joseph's shoes. What are you feeling? Anxiety? Or is there a deeply felt acceptance that this is how it has to be?

And so they head to Bethlehem. Mary and Joseph trek onward in the company of their family and countrymen. All of them depict for us the refugee somberly traveling against his will. What are their faces and steps telling you? The paradox is so striking: they walk because of a mandate issued by the earthly authority, Cesar Augustus. Yet they are oblivious to the fact that Jesus, the King of the universe, moves with them. True redemption is amongst them. How beautifully obscure and hidden grace can be!

Finally, Joseph and Mary reach Bethlehem, but the arrival is bittersweet. We sense that for them the entrance into the town of Joseph's lineage is wrapped in relief, exhaustion, perplexed embarrassment, awkwardness, and perhaps even shame.

Joseph can read his relatives' minds. "You weren't supposed to get your betrothed pregnant!" How can they explain the holiness of their predicament? Where could they even start? They don't. Mary and Joseph keep trusting in God.

What are your most painful experiences of being misunderstood?

Going Deeper

When we reflect on this story, two threads capture our attention: the journey to Bethlehem and Jesus' advent into the midst of oppression, chaos, and rejection. Let's take a moment to reflect on both of them.

God uses the obligatory registration to get Mary and Joseph to the place where they need to be. It is a painful move, but so right, as it was prophesied long ago.

How have life's circumstances forced you to move? Did you feel Jesus traveling with you on that dusty and unpleasant road? Maybe you did not recognize His enigmatic presence then, but can you see it in retrospect?

And yes, Jesus, then as well as now, always comes into the very center of disarray and misery. He comes despite it and because of it. Where has Jesus been "born" into your situation of shame, rejection, or a very deep hurt?

I, Liena, will always remember the most painful and the most joyful day of my life tied together in an ironic knot. On the day of discovering the most severe betrayal, my life shattered into many pieces. Still I had to show up for the night shift of chaplaincy. Every fiber in me shook as I made my way to the hospital where I worked. The first call of the night was to Labor and Delivery.

I walked into the room of a couple who I knew. They placed their newborn daughter into my arms. "We named her Liena."

I took the child, pressed her against my chest, and heard God speaking through my own tears. "I will give you a new life."

That's Bethlehem. "The Word became flesh and made his dwelling among us. We have seen his glory, the glory of the one and only Son, who came from the Father, full of grace and truth" (John 1:14).

How have you experienced new life being born out of circumstances of death?

Prayer for the Journey
Thank You, Jesus, that You come; You make Yourself visible even in the obscurity. Bless me with true discernment of Your faithful presence despite the situation. Amen.

Your Response
What do you appreciate most deeply about God's ways after reading today's story and traveling with Mary and Joseph? Take a moment to reflect and journal.

Looking forward to being with you again,
Your sisters

The Paradox of Limitation

Dear Advent Companion,

Are you ready to travel back in time? Today's Scripture transfers us into the pre-incarnational era of Jesus' life. Next, we witness the most significant change in Jesus' life: He becomes flesh. What does this significant cosmic shift mean for you personally? Let your heart be touched by the wonder of the incarnation.

Preparing to Reflect

"Every good and perfect gift is from above, coming down from the Father of the heavenly lights, who does not change like shifting shadows" (James 1:17). The Father always extends His hand to bless those who will humbly receive the gifts He offers. As I am preparing to immerse myself into today's Scriptures, can I center myself for a few minutes and behold the image of God extending His hand to me? How do I find my hands? Open or clenched? If my hands are clamped shut in fear, mistrust, or hesitation, can I slowly open them to receive what He has to offer me today?

Prayer

"Dear God, I am so afraid to open my clenched fists! Who will I be when I have nothing left to hold on to? Who will I be when I stand before you with empty hands? Please help me to gradually open my hands and to discover that I am not what I own, but what you want to give me." [Henri J.M. Nouwen, *The Only Necessary Thing: Living a Prayerful Life*]

Story of the Day

In the beginning was the Word, and the Word was with God, and the Word was God. He was with God in the beginning.

The Word became flesh and made his dwelling among us. We have seen his glory, the glory of the one and only Son, who came from the Father, full of grace and truth (John 1:1–2, 14).

Entering the Scene

In my study I, Liena, have a Rublev's icon of the Holy Trinity gathered around a shared meal. I have added words under it: "At the heart of the universe is a communion of love." Isn't that our consolation and peace in this tumultuous world? The overflow of love in the life of the Holy Trinity results in the biggest outreach to humanity ever: Jesus descending into flesh.

Incarnation is the most drastic transition from limitless, infinite, and glorious existence to restricted, limited, and finite human life. We can have only a feeble sense of Jesus' experience in the light of the drastic changes of our own lives. What have been your most traumatic experiences of going from glory to landing on the hard ground? Have you experienced the shift of being very healthy to extremely weakened by a major illness, from having a position of power and influence to being stripped of everything, or from experiencing relative freedom to complete imprisonment? Jesus understands them firsthand.

Jesus' incarnation is as difficult and sacrificial as His crucifixion: a giving of oneself away in love. "God's Son descended so that we might ascend, that we might share the divinity of him who humbled himself to share our humanity." [Michael Casey, *Fully Human, Fully Divine: An Interactive Christology*]

Let's look deeper into this divine exchange story.

Going Deeper

How can you really know that someone loves you? Love comprises two very significant components: self-revelation and joyful sacrifice. In Jesus we see them both: the Father's unveiled heart and Jesus' deliberate choice of human limitations for the sake of our expansion and glory. "Christ became human so that we might become divine, that we might see and learn from him the infinitude of love of which the human heart is capable." [Michael Casey, *Fully Human, Fully Divine: An Interactive Christology*]

Jesus leaves the life of glory and enters a vulnerable human existence. We know that someone coming from a position of glory can offer us endless love. Yet the paradox is that the limitation of entering human life reveals the greater depth of His love. The sacrifice of His position shows how much He is willing to give.

How has this been true in your life? How have the constraints that come with sacrifice and suffering revealed someone's love for you or your love for them?

Jesus' intention is clear: to free our hearts of ever doubting God's love and to invite us into true communion with the Trinity. Since only vulnerability creates a true union of hearts, Jesus unveils God's open heart to us. "Anyone who has seen me has seen the Father" (John 14:9). "The Son is the radiance of God's glory and the exact representation of his being" (Hebrews 1:3).

St. John of the Cross offers a beautiful image to describe God's vulnerability in Jesus: "His heart an open wound with love" [*The Collected Works of St. John of the Cross*] Jesus opens Himself up to human love and also to misunderstanding, scorn, ridicule, and ultimately crucifixion to bridge the human heart to God's heart. He pays for His emotional and spiritual exposure; yet it gains for us wide, privileged communion with God as He truly is.

What has your journey been of reciprocating God's "open wound with love"? What has God been teaching you about the power of vulnerability in your other relationships?

Prayer for the Journey
Father, thank You for the gift of Jesus who unveils Your heart to me. Amen.

Your Response
How do Brené Brown's words speak to you? "Staying vulnerable is a risk we have to take if we want to experience connection." [*Daring Greatly: How the Courage to Be Vulnerable Transforms the Way We Live*]

Journal and pray about your fears of opening up to God and others.

Entrusting you into the love of God,
Jacqueline and Liena

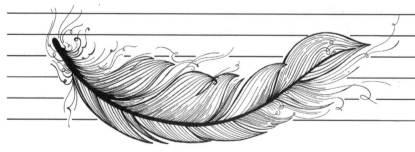

God Is Trusting You

Dear Advent Companion,

We hear plenty about our need to trust God. But have you ever thought of God trusting you? What if God is saying the same about you as He did about Moses? "He is the one I trust" (Numbers 12:7 NLT). How would that change your relationship with God and with all who are entrusted to you? How would that touch your heart? Let God's trust expressed in today's Scripture energize and inspire you.

Preparing to Reflect

God is faithfully with me, but more, I am created in His image with unimaginable potential for so much good. I am truly made through Him and for Him.

In preparation to pray, I still myself and connect with God's heartbeat within me and His hope for this world through me. I make an intention to be open to His Word and work today. I place my hand upon my heart, the sign of God's sustaining presence within me. Can I descend into my spirit to pray?

Prayer

"When I consider your heavens, the work of your fingers, the moon and the stars, which you have set in place, what is mankind that you are mindful of them, human beings that you care for them? You have made them a little lower than the angels and crowned them with glory and honor" (Psalm 8:3–5). Thank You. Amen.

Story of the Day

While they were there, the time came for the baby to be born, and she gave birth to her firstborn, a son. She wrapped him in cloths and placed him in a manger (Luke 2:6–7).

Entering the Scene

Place yourself in the corner of the stable. What do you see? Are the animals wandering about you in this strange scene? A couple labors together to bring a new life into this world. We witness pushing, moaning, and groaning until the wet, warm bundle of God's gift slides into Joseph's arms. God watches His Son being born for the first time.

Joseph and Mary are also watching. What is it like for Mary to see God gazing at her through the eyes of the child formed of her own flesh? Does He look anything like her? What is it like for Joseph to become a father to a Son of the most mystical origins?

Mary wraps Jesus in swaddling cloths and lays Him in the manger: the only place the world has spared for the Son of God.

Going Deeper

When preparing for Christmas Eve worship service, I, Liena, placed a little manger at the altar. I filled it with hay and put a wooden cross in Christ's cradle.

My mom asked, "Why is this cross there on the night of Christ's birth?"

I replied, "That is what Mary saw when she placed Him in the manger that holy night."

> The description of His birth in the Gospel doesn't say that she held Him in her arms but that she "wrapped Him in swaddling clothes and laid Him in the manger." As if her first act was to lay Him on the Cross. She knew that this little son of hers was God's Son and that God had not given Him to her for herself alone but for the whole world. She knew, better than anyone else will ever know it, that the greatest of all griefs is to be unable to mitigate the suffering of one whom we love. But she was willing to suffer that, because that was what He asked of her. [Caryll Houselander, *The Reed of God: A New Edition of a Spiritual Classic*]

But for now, until the day of His Cross, she would take care of Him as she already had: carrying and nurturing Him in her body. She would honor the trust God had shown to her. God's trust in us human beings is so profoundly humbling. I recall a friend of mine changing her grandchild's diapers and thinking of the Christ child: His vulnerability in human hands. God chooses to trust us. Why? His loving trust and vulnerability disarm our hearts and express His belief in His image in us. Nothing is more powerful for our motivation to be the best we can ever be. In responding to God's trust we bloom and fulfill our highest calling.

Since God empowers us by trusting us, I love to show my trust in people, even at my own risk. The pleasure of seeing someone's heart change and bloom under this trust is spiritually thrilling. How does God call you to express trust? Who and what has He entrusted to you?

Prayer for the Journey

Thank You, Lord, for Your trust in me. May my life be an ever-increasing joyful partnership with Your humility. Amen.

Your Response

How do you think of yourself after today's reflection? Tell God about your impressions. Pray and journal your heart.

With loving thoughts,
Liena and Jacqueline

Making Space for Jesus

Dear Advent Friend,

You might have read different Scriptures encouraging hospitality in your life. Consider these words: "Always be eager to practice hospitality" (Romans 12:13 NLT). How do you seek to welcome others not only into your home but also into your heart? What is the most meaningful way someone has ever welcomed you? Today's reflection encourages us to open the gift of hospitality anew. Would you unwrap this treasure with us?

Preparing to Reflect

God treasures His communion with me. Can I close my eyes and imagine Christ as my friend sitting across from me and lovingly asking me, "How are you?"

What is my answer?

He continues, "How may I serve you today?"

I open my deepest needs to Him now.

Prayer

Christ, my loving Friend, teach me to welcome You as You welcome me. Amen.

Story of the Day
There was no room for them in the inn (Luke 2:7 KJV).

Entering the Scene

Oh, little town of Bethlehem, you are a loud bazaar this holy night. People and their troubles crowd your narrow streets. Travelers brush shoulders while pushing their way through to registration. Survival, food, and shelter consume people's minds. One could only dream to find a still and quiet place in the midst of this chaos. What a confusing time for a woman to be in labor!

Imagine yourself being an innkeeper at this busy and advantageous time for business. Where would your focus be?

It is not surprising that Mary and Joseph are squeezed out in the swarm of people's many needs. They must be relieved to find a humble but solitary place to usher their son into this world.

Has the Father removed Mary and Joseph from the hustle of the town and the curious stares of distant relatives and immediate family? Does He preserve a moment of peace in which to bring Jesus obscurely into this world? "The psalmist had hymned Christ's coming on harps of gold. The prophets had foretold it with burning tongues. But now the loudest telling of His presence on earth is to be the heartbeat within the heartbeat of a child." [Caryll Houselander, *The Reed of God: A New Edition of a Spiritual Classic*]

Jesus is like a hidden treasure to be found only by those who earnestly seek Him in the most unusual places even in the dark of the night and the remoteness of a stable.

Do you want to be the one? Do you long to make a cradle for Him in your own heart?

Going Deeper

Mary is the first to show us how to welcome Jesus. She embodies true hospitality. By saying yes to God's proposal through the angel Gabriel, her body becomes the chalice that holds the Son of God. And now her hands hold the Bread of Life to be given away into this world. How does this inspire you to welcome Jesus as the indwelling Holy Spirit into your own being and then share Him with others?

True hospitality stretches wider than the opened door of our house to welcome friends or strangers. A full welcome makes space for others in the shelter of our hearts. This invitation can only be extended through the intricate work of compassionate listening.

> To listen is very hard, because it asks of us so much interior stability that we no longer need to prove ourselves by speeches, arguments, statements, or declarations. True listeners no longer have an inner need to make their presence known. They are to receive, to welcome, to accept.
>
> Listening is much more than allowing another to talk while waiting for a chance to respond. Listening is paying full attention to others and welcoming them into our very beings. The beauty of listening is that, those who are listened to start feeling accepted, start taking their words more seriously and discovering their own true selves. Listening is a form of spiritual hospitality by which you invite strangers to become friends, to get to know their inner selves more fully, and even to dare to be silent with you. [Henri J. M. Nouwen, *Bread for the Journey: A Daybook of Wisdom and Faith*]

Isn't true hospitality of heart the gift that many long for on a daily basis and especially during the holiday season? During this time of the year people feel the loneliest and are impacted the most by difficult family dynamics. Is God inviting you in any way to pause in the midst of your busyness and take a loving look around you to see who needs to be welcomed into your heart this Advent season? We welcome Jesus into this world through the doorway of our own open hearts. This might be the most valuable gift we can offer to people in our lives.

Hospitality is never a one-way gift. The guests of our hearts leave treasures behind. Working with patients and their families, I, Liena, learned this lesson long ago: God feeds me with the same hand I feed others.

What are some of the gifts you have received in this Advent season from people who have stayed in the sanctuary of your heart?

Prayer for the Journey

Lord, make my heart a sanctuary for You and others. Free me from all fears and hesitations. Turn the imperfections of my inner space into shared human connections. Amen.

Your Response

How do you desire to apply today's Scriptures in your life? Assign words to your intentions as you journal and express them in prayer.

With God's peace,
Your friends

The Fourth Week of Advent

Outcast No More

Dear Fellow Pilgrim,

Today we will join the shepherds and walk in their sandals for a moment.

Have you ever felt marginalized? There have been times in our lives that we have experienced it because of being a woman, a foreigner, or a person of color.

Not only do the shepherds receive smirks and frowns, but also the nature of their work keeps them from participating in religious and social activities. Theirs is a life of constant movement draped in a distinct kind of loneliness. Have they accepted the status quo, expecting nothing more than being a social outcast? Most likely, but God has not designed this destiny for them. He has a great surprise and honor in store for them.

Try to enter into this story with new eyes—the eyes of the shepherds. What does God reveal to you?

Preparing to Reflect

The psalmist says, "Because he bends down to listen, I will pray as long as I have breath!" (Psalm 116:2 NLT). I close my eyes and breathe in gratitude for His intentionality towards me. God is bending down to listen to me. Can I stay with this image for few minutes?

Prayer

Though You, oh Lord, are exalted, You look so kindly on the lowly. Your heart is with the least of us, and Your grace is profoundly rich toward us. I accept Your humility and love toward me. Amen.

Story of the Day:

And there were shepherds living out in the fields nearby, keeping watch over their flocks at night. An angel of the Lord appeared to them, and the glory of the Lord shone around them, and they were terrified. But the angel said to them, "Do not be afraid. I bring you good news that will cause great joy for all the people. Today in the town of David a Savior has been born to you; he is the Messiah, the Lord. This will be a sign to you: You will find a baby wrapped in cloths and lying in a manger" (Luke 2:8–12).

Entering the Scene

The night has fallen. Stillness and drowsiness set in. The sheep rest and the familiar nighttime sounds slowly saturate the air. The flames of the bonfire do a listless dance and shadows fall on those asleep by the fire. Some shepherds sleep while others take turns keeping watch over the flock, protecting them from thieves and wild animals. Imagine being one of them. What do you sense about your surroundings? How does it feel to lead a life of ongoing homelessness under God's wide sky?

Suddenly a light, brighter than the sun, slashes and transforms the darkness. A river of glorious light streams down from heaven. All are taken aback, terrified, and speechless. If you were one of them, what would you be feeling in this moment? Have you ever experienced the glory of the Lord?

This is only the beginning! An angel appears before you in an attempt to bring comfort: "Do not be afraid. I bring you good news." What is your response to the introduction of the gospel?

Going Deeper

How often does one experience the glory of the Lord and receive a message from an angel? Ironically, the shepherds, who are considered the scum of the earth, are greatly privileged this night. God chooses them to rejoice in the birth of His Son and welcome Him with singularly focused hearts.

The shepherds become a living icon of the message just proclaimed from above: there is good news for all people, for God's favor rests on us through Christ.

Furthermore, this story challenges us to recognize the people in our lives of whom we think as unworthy to receive grace. It reminds us of the parable where Jesus challenges his disciples, "Are you envious because I am generous?" (Matthew 20:15).

There is not only good news for all people, but also for all of who and what we are. So many times we reject and despise our shadow side similar to the shepherds. Will you let Him embrace "the shepherd" within you?

Prayer

Lord, reveal Your glory to me. I want to know You, as You truly are, in all of Your magnificence, beauty, and power. Amen.

Your Response

Tell Jesus about the "shepherd" in you. Allow Him to respond to you. Journal your thoughts and what you think His response is to you.

May grace multiply in your life,
Your sisters in Christ

Do You Want to Worship with Heaven?

Our Dear Friend,

This next reading reminds us of a cornucopia bursting with divine love. There is no end to God's generosity. Have you ever been in a situation where one blessing was given on top of another blessing and you were almost overwhelmed by it all? God's goodness stuns the shepherds. Keep your heart open and let God's divine bounty transform you as it transforms them.

Preparing to Reflect

The Scripture urges us to "enter his gates with thanksgiving and his courts with praise" (Psalm 100:4). I start my prayer and reflection time by looking back at the past day or week. What am I grateful for?

Prayer

Our loving God, You are generous and without end. I thank You. Help me to be open to Your gifts. Carve in me a perfect receptacle of Your outpouring grace. Amen.

Story of the Day

Suddenly a great company of the heavenly host appeared with the angel, praising God and saying, "Glory to God in the highest heaven, and on earth peace to those on whom his favor rests (Luke 2:13–14).

Entering the Scene

The revelation keeps on deepening. We invite you to stay with this discovery. The curtains of another dimension are drawn back, and we see the stage of heaven in splendid worship.

The heavenly hosts and the Lord's army give full recognition to the Father's glory in heaven and His work on earth. The heavenly church sings praises to our living God for this marvelous plan of salvation.

The shepherds stand there like the apostle John, jaw dropped, when he received God's great revelation of heavenly realms. This is how John describes his experience: "After this I looked, and there before me was a door standing open in heaven. . . . Day and night they never stop saying: 'Holy, holy, holy is the Lord God Almighty, who was, and is, and is to come'" (Revelation 4:1, 8).

Imagine yourself with the shepherds that unusual night. What is it like to witness this usually concealed heavenly reality unveiled before your very eyes? Are you awestruck, encouraged, humbled, or otherwise touched? It is a holy night of a heavenly feast spilling down to earth. Remain there for a while and receive it.

Going Deeper

What does this open gate to heaven's splendor actually intend to convey to the shepherds—to all of us? The message is compelling: the unity between heaven and earth is accomplished through the birth of Christ. Yes, heaven and earth are married this holy night. Jesus becomes the living bridge between these two realms.

"For there is one God and one mediator between God and mankind, the man Christ Jesus" (1 Timothy 2:5). He reconciles us with the Father, and He conquers the war inside us. There is a promise for peace in our relationship with God and with our own hearts. Can you claim this promise?

It does not stop there. You and I are invited to be part of Christ's ministry. "All this is from God, who reconciled us to himself through Christ and gave us the ministry of reconciliation: that God was reconciling the world to himself in Christ, not counting people's sins against them. And he has committed to us the message of reconciliation. We are therefore Christ's ambassadors, as though God were making his appeal through us" (2 Corinthians 5:18–20).

What does the "ministry of reconciliation" look like in your life? How are you called to be a *bridge* between people and God, between one person and another, between different groups of people? Perhaps you are to be the bridge between seemingly opposite things inside your own world and heart. Ponder for a moment and notice if there are any thoughts along this line stirring inside you.

Prayer for the Journey
Lord, help me to tap into the joy of heavenly celebration over Christ's work of reconciliation in this world. Equip me to be Your Son's ambassador wherever I am placed. Amen.

Your Response
How does this scene of heavenly worship or anything else in this story touch you? To what is the Father inviting you? Please journal, pray, and reflect.

Love,
Your companions in Christ

A Heavenly Upgrade

God's Beloved,

Today's passage invites us to experience a thrill, sheer delight, and innocent joy. It calls for movement on our part, rushing forward with the shepherds toward Bethlehem. And it reminds us of those times in our lives when we can hardly wait to share our excitement with anyone who will listen. Today, you are invited into the pursuit of the divine. Unleash your heart and follow it.

Preparing to Reflect

A lively and deep desire is a form of prayer. I close my eyes and connect with my desire for God and His embrace. Can I envision myself running toward the Lord? I allow the Lord to pick me up and twirl me around. His face explodes with laughter. I stay with this image and take it in.

Prayer

Lord, I so desire to be Your child, holding nothing back and plunging into Your arms. Give me complete freedom toward You. Amen.

Story of the Day

When the angels had left them and gone into heaven, the shepherds said to one another, "Let's go to Bethlehem and see this thing that has happened, which the Lord has told us about."

So they hurried off and found Mary and Joseph, and the baby, who was lying in the manger. When they had seen him, they spread the word concerning what had been told them about this child, and all who heard it were amazed at what the shepherds said to them. The shepherds returned, glorifying and praising God for all the things they had heard and seen, which were just as they had been told (Luke 2:15–18, 20).

Entering the Scene

"Let's go! Let's hurry!" The shepherds take us by the hand to lead us deeper into the story of Christ's birth. Let's run like enthused and free children. Our feet touch the grass and our bodies brush against the sheep. What's next?

Mary and Joseph hear a noise coming nearer to them—a mixture of human and animal sounds. What is this all about, they wonder?

And then, here we are. All our eyes are nailed to this sight: the manger with a baby wrapped in swaddling cloths. Each shepherd whispers to himself, "It's true what the angels have proclaimed!"

What is this moment like for you? Only a limited few and the lowly witness the birth of God's Son.

Going Deeper

Mary's prophecy about God exalting the lowly comes true before her own eyes. The Virgin surely remembers that she said, "His mighty arm has done tremendous things! He has scattered the proud and haughty ones. He has brought down princes from their thrones and exalted the humble" (Luke 1:51-52 NLT). Here the humble shepherds stand, blessed with the revelation from the heavenly host and the sight of the Savior. In them we see how low and fully God bends to reach the "bottom" of society's barrel. Surely salvation is for all.

The shepherds become the first evangelists ever. Touched and transformed by their encounter with the divine, their joy is uncontainable. Silence would be deadly to them. These simple men go into the streets or wherever a human soul can be found to proclaim the truly Good News. "When they had seen him, they spread the word concerning what had been told them about this child, and all who heard it were amazed at what the shepherds said to them" (Luke 2:17–18). This kind of enthusiasm is only born of a very personal encounter with the living God. Have you ever experienced something similar in your own life?

Does everyone believe the shepherds? Most likely not; however, all are amazed. Not a trace of indifference. The shepherds unknowingly give us an example of how joy is the tool for evangelizing. No words of God's punishment or wrath are muttered. Only God's goodness is lifted up. Can we stay in the shepherds' shoes to bring the Gospel to others?

Does their spreading of the word continue for years? When you have an uneventful shepherd's life and an experience like this comes along, it becomes the center of your existence.

Do the shepherds follow the life of Jesus and maybe even hear Him say one day, "I am the good shepherd. The good shepherd lays down his life for the sheep" (John 10:11)? What an honor for them to hear Jesus identifying with their lives.

Prayer for the Journey

My loving God, I long for life-changing encounters with You. Make my joy uncontainable and my witness natural in this world. Amen.

Your Response
What does the shepherds' story evoke in you? Pray your heart and journal your observations.

Sincerely,
Your loving friends

What Are You Treasuring in Your Heart?

Dear Friend,

Do you ever remember dropping a rock into a deep well? You hear one initial plop and then silence, but you know that's not the end. The stone keeps sinking deeper and deeper into the water. So it happens with Mary.

Only one short sentence describes the way she reacts to the shepherds' visit and message: "Mary treasured up all these things and pondered them in her heart" (Luke 2:19). However, we know so much more transpires. Mary responds with silence and contemplation because "the current of her soul flows far deeper to bubble forth its emotions." [Bishop Samuel Wilberforce, *The Biblical Illustrator*] What messages have you heard thus far this Advent season that have had a similar effect on you?

Preparing to Reflect

"Love to pray, since prayer enlarges the heart until it is capable to contain God's gift of Himself. Ask and seek and your heart will grow big enough to receive Him and keep Him as your own." [Mother Teresa] To prepare for prayer and reflection, I become aware of my breathing and remember that the Holy Spirit in Hebrew is *Ruah godsheka,* the breath of God. With each breath I take, I imagine the Lord expanding my heart and filling it with His glorious presence to abide with me forever.

Prayer

"May these words of my mouth and this meditation of my heart be pleasing in your sight, LORD, my Rock and my Redeemer" (Psalm 19:14).

Story of the Day

But Mary treasured up all these things and pondered them in her heart.

On the eighth day, when it was time to circumcise the child, he was named Jesus, the name the angel had given him before he was conceived (Luke 2:19, 21).

Entering the Scene

The word *pondering* in Greek literally means "bringing together" or "bearing together." We can see all the people and heavenly beings who have brought forth a prophecy about her Son's destiny lining up before the Virgin's internal eye: Gabriel, Elizabeth, her own husband, and the shepherds. She has been given many threads to weave together into a tapestry of deeper understanding.

As you quietly watch Mary dropping down deeper and deeper into her heart, what do you sense about her and her silence? To us this silence feels pregnant, humble, and acquiescent.

The contemplations of her heart result in obedient responses. As commanded, she names her son Jesus at His circumcision, which means "Yahweh saves."

Going Deeper

"When a common nature would have exulted, when vanity would have babbled, or when common wonder and doubt would have gone asking for explanations, it is said of her, 'Mary kept all these things and pondered them in her heart.'" [A.G. Mercer, D.D., *The Biblical Illustrator*]

We need to allow time for our significant life experiences to settle into our beings. Following Mary's example, might we simply be still before God and our own souls instead of reacting or announcing our experiences to the world? Stillness provides the necessary time and space for stormy waters to calm as we wait for insight and discernment to emerge from deep within.

Mary in her wisdom lets the question, "What does this mean?" speak to her. What is your usual reaction to anything joyous, upsetting, or perplexing in your life?

Mary hears recurrently, from many different sources, prophetic words about her son's destiny. The messengers are many: the angel, Elizabeth, Anna, Simeon, the shepherds, the wise men, and her husband, through his affirmative actions. Why isn't once enough? The Holy Spirit displays a strong and persistent pattern. He revisits our hearts with the same message to draw our attention and to build up our faith.

Now ponder your own life. What promptings or call keep revisiting you again and again? Maybe you have been too busy or too scared to finally welcome the guest who always speaks of God's dream for you and your own deepest desire. We pray with you for determination, strength, and courage to heed God's invitation and let it finally materialize in your life.

Prayer for the Journey

Holy Spirit, You are so patient but also so determined to knock at the door of our hearts until we respond. Give us the courage, strength, and humility to live out the Father's will. Amen.

Your Response

Take some time to pray and journal on those promptings which you have heard repeatedly and which require a response. What would it take for them to materialize in your life?

With prayer for your highest good,
Liena and Jacqueline

Waiting Well

Hello,

Would you say you are a patient person? Do you wait well? If we are honest, most of us would say that we struggle when our gratification must be put on hold. Initially as we wait, we might be able to convince ourselves that we will see the fruit of our patience.

Yet, if our waiting lasts for years, our patience wanes. Even though hope befriends us in our waiting, our questions persist. Why isn't there any progress? When will things change? How much longer? Has He forgotten me? Everyone who waits questions.

Come discover with us what it is like to wait for years on end and to see the Lord bring sweet consolation.

Preparing to Reflect

"I wait for the Lord more than watchmen wait for the morning, more than watchmen wait for the morning" (Psalm 130:6). With morning comes light, an ease and relief from tension. When light is present, the enemy can't move so freely any longer. Can I open my body, soul, and spirit to God's light and feel the relief of His presence, protection, and peace? I let myself bathe in His light and goodness. I am well because He is with me.

Prayer

Lord, Your presence is peace everlasting and a sweet relief from all of my fears. I entrust all my worries and my unfolding life to You. I simply rest in You and Your sense of timing. Amen.

Story of the Day

When the time came for the purification rites required by the Law of Moses, Joseph and Mary took him to Jerusalem to present him to the Lord (as it is written in the Law of the Lord, "Every firstborn male is to be consecrated to the Lord"), and to offer a sacrifice in keeping with what is said in the Law of the Lord: "a pair of doves or two young pigeons."

Now there was a man in Jerusalem called Simeon, who was righteous and devout. He was waiting for the consolation of Israel, and the Holy Spirit was on him. It had been revealed to him by the Holy Spirit that he would not die before he had seen the Lord's Messiah. Moved by the Spirit, he went into the temple courts (Luke 2:22–27).

Entering the Scene

Mary and Joseph have been eagerly waiting for this day. Do you remember waiting for a dedication or a baptism of your own child or a child you cared for?

Jesus' parents are not the only ones to wait. Simeon, an old prophet, has been patiently waiting for many years to lock eyes with Israel's Savior.

God arranges a divine meeting for Simeon as Joseph and Mary make their way to the temple. They go in joyful obedience. Meanwhile the Holy Spirit moves Simeon into this monumental meeting.

Let's watch for the curtain to be drawn.

Going Deeper

The Holy Spirit promised Simeon he would not die before seeing the Lord's Christ. Does the old man ever wonder if he truly will see this Christ as the pains and aches of his aged body start to set in? Maybe the opposite is true: as Simeon's dying approaches, his confidence in the fulfillment of God's promise increases.

How does one wait well without losing heart, falling into resentment, or giving into passivity? What do you do as you wait? All three—Simeon, Zechariah, and Elizabeth—indicate the way: they stay steeped and unmoved in their devotion to the Lord in spite of unfulfilled dreams and the ticking of time. While circumstances swirl around them like a stinging wind, they remain firmly rooted in the God they know. Nothing changes their devotion to their Beloved. They stay faithful to the ordinary duties of life until the extraordinary comes.

Simeon waits, but not in a passive idleness. He awaits God's coming in a spirit of prayer, keen attunement to the Spirit's voice, and quiet watchfulness.

Waiting is active. Most of us think of waiting as something very passive, a hopeless state determined by events totally out of our hands. But there is none of this passivity in Scripture. Those who are waiting are waiting very actively. They know that what they are waiting for is growing from the ground on which they are standing. That's the secret. The secret of waiting is the fact that the seed has been planted, that something has begun. Active waiting means to be present fully to the moment, in the conviction that something is happening. A waiting person is a patient person. [Henri J. M. Nouwen, *The Path of Waiting*]

Are you actively engaged in your waiting: looking for the signs of God's goodness in your daily life? Life in faith is always a joyful anticipation and recognition of His coming.

Prayer for the Journey

Lord, help me to be fully engaged with You and my daily life as I wait for the coming of the extraordinary. Amen.

Your Response

What has God been teaching you about waiting? What is your response to Simeon's journey?

Love and peace,
Jacqueline and Liena

Embracing Your Salvation

Dear Fellow Traveler,

We know that God is constantly communicating with us. Since we are often distracted, we may not always acknowledge or hear Him. Yet, once in a while when the Holy Spirit nudges us, we are keenly aware, and we move into the space into which He is leading us.

In today's story, Simeon has just such an experience. What happens as he listens, obeys, and enters into that space in which the Holy Spirit is inviting him?

Preparing to Reflect

In the Gospel of Luke we read how Jesus opens His disciples' minds so that they can understand the Scriptures (see Luke 24:13–32). I still myself now and ask the Lord to open my understanding of His words of life for me today.

Prayer

Lord, I want to hear You, listen to You, and obey You. Lead me today in this time of prayer into that sweet place with You. Amen.

Story of the Day

When the parents brought in the child Jesus to do for him what the custom of the Law required, Simeon took him in his arms and praised God, saying:

"Sovereign Lord, as you have promised,
    you may now dismiss your servant in peace.
For my eyes have seen your salvation,
    which you have prepared in the sight of all nations:
a light for revelation to the Gentiles,
    and the glory of your people Israel."

The child's father and mother marveled at what was said about him (Luke 2:27–33).

Entering the Scene

Mary and Joseph get that uncomfortable feeling that someone is staring at them. You know the feeling. People crowd the temple, yet an individual in this throng singles them out and eyes them intensely. They turn to get a look at this person and notice he is now moving toward them.

What do they see in him? The old prophet is timeworn, but there is fire in his eyes. He seems to almost leap toward them with outstretched hands. His gaze is fixed on their son. How would you feel as the parent?

He feels like a friend, but he is a stranger. Even so, Mary places Jesus into Simeon's wrinkled arms. He embraces Jesus with the greatest affection imaginable and lays him on his bosom, near his heart. Precious treasure found at last. Tears stream into the crevices of his face; his head and eyes move heavenward. The words start to flow: "Sovereign Lord, as you have promised. . . ."

Going Deeper

Isn't it beautiful that the name Simeon comes from the words *listening* and *hearing*? It might appear a small thing to follow an inner prompting to head toward the temple. However, it turns out to be the most transformative one. He meets his Savior. You never know which day will hold the biggest of God's surprises. Can you think of responding to a specific prompting by the Holy Spirit that turned out to be a divine appointment or a life-altering event? Take a moment to give thanks.

When Simeon sees Christ, he claims Him. It is not just enough to know that salvation has come, to witness it from afar, or even to admire it from a distance. Redemption has to be held close to his heart. What does it mean for you to embrace your salvation with your entire being and then to proclaim it?

Simeon is an amazingly graceful New Testament saint, displaying a strong sense of timing. He acknowledges a new era dawning, even for the Gentiles, and he is able to let his own life go. "Now dismiss your servant in peace." Believing and receiving God's promise always welcomes us into His rest.

I, Liena, have seen many deaths. What a blessing to see someone die with this kind of resolution and peace. What needs to happen in your life and in your soul for you to have a complete peace and contentment about your own dying? What still feels unfinished, not embraced, and not held close enough to your heart?

Prayer for the Journey

Instead of a verbal prayer, imagine yourself being in Simeon's place. Mary puts Jesus into your arms. Stay with this image for a while and let your salvation be so close to your heart.

Your Response
How does it feel to hold Jesus? Journal your thoughts.

Wishing you Advent joy,
Liena and Jacqueline

Can A Blessing Pierce Your Soul?

Dear Friend,

As you drive through your neighborhood at this time of year, you might see illuminated figurines of the holy family. Perhaps your place of worship has a crèche on the altar. In each setting, every figure is turned toward Jesus.

At Advent, we, too, focus on the Christ child. God in His wisdom chose to enter into our world and our lives in the form of a baby. Yet our text today reminds us that at some point we will need to encounter the man Jesus. We will not be able to ignore the ultimate reason why the Father sent his Son. What might this encounter look like for you this Advent?

Preparing to Reflect

"My soul thirsts for God, for the living God" (Psalm 42:2). I gently lay aside all distractions and let myself dwell for a moment on the deepest spiritual thirst within me. What is it? I take time to recognize it. I let this sacred longing for God now arise within me like the tide, seeping into every cell of my being. Can this desire become my offering to God as I am about to pray?

Prayer

Lord, I lay down any apprehensions I might have about encountering You today. Come and water any parched ground in my heart right now. Amen.

Story of the Day

And Simeon blessed them and said to Mary His mother, "Behold, this Child is appointed for the fall and rise of many in Israel, and for a sign to be opposed— and a sword will pierce even your own soul—to the end that thoughts from many hearts may be revealed" (Luke 2:34–35 NASB).

Entering the Scene

Take yourself to where Mary is, standing before Simeon. Imagine the two of you watching his heart moved with deep emotion as he proclaims this little child is "the Lord's salvation" and "the glory of Israel." He blesses the holy family.

Next he makes a statement that no one is quite ready to hear. Many will oppose and reject this beloved child. Jesus will become the stumbling block for those dismissing Him as the Messiah. Along the way, Mary's heart will be pierced also.

How is Mary receiving this news? Shaking her head in disbelief, being simply too stunned, or accepting this double-sided prophecy without comment? What is a mother supposed to do with these weighty words spoken over her child? As an observer, how do you want to comfort Mary?

Going Deeper

One day, at the foot of her Son's cross, Mary will remember Simeon's words of a sword piercing her soul. Now these words feel so troublesome and harsh, but then maybe they will become oddly comforting, assigning purpose and meaning to her suffering.

I frequently witness what patients and their families can endure and withstand if they see a purpose and can find a redemptive value in their hardships. Viktor E. Frankl speaks of his own experience after surviving a concentration camp: "In some ways suffering ceases to be suffering at the moment it finds a meaning, such as the meaning of a sacrifice." [*Man's Search for Meaning*] If you are suffering this Advent, how are you called to assign meaning to your pain with the comfort and insight of the Holy Spirit?

The purpose of Mary's passion is rather unusual: a sword will pierce her soul so that the truth of many hearts may be uncovered. What exactly is this prophecy getting at? The way we react to the cross of Jesus and those suffering with Him exposes the state of our hearts. Our response to Jesus determines our falling or rising. There is no room for ambivalence here. How does this challenge you?

Prayer for the Journey

Lord Jesus, as I look at Your meaningful cross and Your mother's anguish, help me to find significance and purpose in my own suffering. Amen.

Your Response

What is your relationship to Jesus right now? Pray and journal your thoughts about how you would like this relationship to grow.

Healing to you,
Your Advent companions

From Christmas to Epiphany

Admirable Devotion

Dear Companion,

Do you have someone in your faith community or someone you know whose life with God is a marvel to you? Think about this person for a moment. What about this believer's faith walk do you find so captivating?

Anna, the subject of today's story, lives with God in an unusual intimacy. Read with us and discover how she exudes faithfulness and love to God.

Preparing to Reflect

Mary of Bethany made a choice to retreat from life's urgent demands and sit at Jesus' feet ready to be taught. Jesus praised her for her brave preference. "Mary has chosen what is better, and it will not be taken away from her" (Luke 10:42). Can I, too, retreat from everything that has to be done and give my full attention to the Lord now? I imagine sitting at Jesus' feet with Mary: full of expectation and wonder.

Prayer

Loving God, "Better is one day in your courts than a thousand elsewhere" (Psalm 84:10). Your presence is the strength of my heart. Thank You for drawing me into this time of worship and prayer. Amen.

Story of the Day

There was also a prophet, Anna, the daughter of Penuel, of the tribe of Asher. She was very old; she had lived with her husband seven years after her marriage, and then was a widow until she was eighty-four. She never left the temple but worshiped night and day, fasting and praying (Luke 2:36–37).

Entering the Scene

What is your first impression of Anna? We might immediately have deep empathy for her as her marriage ended after such a short time. Yet we can imagine she poured out her grief to God and found joy in praising Him. It is apparent that Anna's life has two distinct seasons: the years of being encircled by her family and her years at the temple. Being so engaged in the rhythm of a devoted life to God, Anna could be considered a monastic of her time.

Anna's name means "grace" and "favor." All her being embodies God's promise: "Even youths grow tired and weary, and young men stumble and fall; but those who hope in the LORD will renew their strength" (Isaiah 40:30–31).

How do you imagine Anna's life at the temple? We notice Anna's shrunken and thin body moving around the temple helping out here and there, and her eyes relentlessly studying the little ones. Can't you just hear her muttering under her breath, "Not yet," "Not this one," "Soon," "Very soon"?

Anna has the growing assurance emerging from fasting and prayer that the salvation of Israel is at hand. What growing assurance do you sense in your spirit about your own life?

Going Deeper

Anna comes from the tribe of Asher, considered one of the lost tribes after the exile in Babylon. Many from the ten "lost" tribes dispersed among the surviving tribes of Judah and Benjamin. Anna represents the life force and resilience of all survivors in the past and in the present. It is fascinating that the blessing her tribe received from Moses is "The bolts of your gates will be iron and bronze, and your strength will equal your days" (Deuteronomy 33:25). Here she is, a survivor of her husband's death and all the hardships that widowhood brings. As you reflect on Anna, what has God's grace empowered you to survive?

Apparently her husband did not have any brothers, for otherwise she would have been obligated to marry one of them to continue her husband's name. Being led by divine providence, she came to the house of the Lord to find refuge and to remain. She has been so vulnerable all of her life, depending on her community, but also so wise to know the deeper truth of "Do not be afraid; you will not be put to shame. . . . You will forget the shame of your youth and remember no more the reproach of your widowhood. For your Maker is your husband" (Isaiah 54:4–5).

Anna has spread out the roots of her devotion so deep like those of an old tree; their roots are inseparable from the soil they have grown in. There is no meaning of life apart from her God. "Whom have I in heaven but you? And earth has nothing I desire besides you" (Psalm 73:25).

Prayer for the Journey

My loving God, only You can establish me "like a tree planted by streams of water, which yields its fruit in season and whose leaf doesn't wither" (Psalm 1:3). This is what I long for. Amen.

Your Response

As you look at Anna's life in today's passage, how could she be a model for you? Express yourself in writing.

Entrusting you in His care,
Liena and Jacqueline

In the Right Place at the Right Time

Hello, Dear One!

As the Advent season progressed, our lives may have picked up the pace. Today may be a good day to slow down, step back, and reassess from where we have come this season and how we want to go forward. The Lord definitely seeks to encounter us. We, too, want to meet with Him. He may long to lead us to the right place at the right time to experience something amazing with Him. Let's take a look at Anna's timely encounter with Jesus, His parents, and Simeon.

Preparing to Reflect

Faithfulness to daily prayer forms in us a habit of being sensitive to the voice of the Holy Spirit when we return to our daily duties. As I spend this time with the Lord, He teaches me to listen. Can I now gently turn from all external distraction and my mind's chatter in order to withdraw into the sanctuary of my heart to meet God who lives and speaks there?

Prayer

Lord, here I am. Your servant is listening to Your guidance today. Amen.

Story of the Day

Coming up to them at that very moment, she gave thanks to God and spoke about the child to all who were looking forward to the redemption of Jerusalem (Luke 2:38).

Entering the Scene

Anna comes up to Joseph, Mary, Simeon, and baby Jesus "at that very moment." What precise and accurate guidance of the Holy Spirit! Reflect with us on those times in your life when you were unmistakably guided to a divine appointment. The awareness of God's faithfulness, exactness, and presence in the smallest details of life gives us such a deep sense of rest and peace.

Anna probably has been waiting for this moment for a long time. She reminds us of St. Monica, the mother of St. Augustine who spent countless years in prayer for Augustine while he was a wild and worldly man. Some prayers are answered quickly, others we must labor over faithfully. Anna's work has been a prayer for the salvation of Israel.

What is prayer like for you? Do you know of any fruit produced by faithful, long-term prayer in your own life or someone else's life?

Going Deeper

Anna's life of worship has undoubtedly attuned her heart to the Holy Spirit. Her life with God is an ocean wave that ebbs only to flow back to shore with greater fullness and strength. Back and forth, back and forth. Anna goes into her inner sanctuary of the heart through the door of prayer and fasting and comes out with a keen ability to recognize God's work of salvation among His people. Living by this rhythm, she adroitly recognizes the Christ child.

Anna's father's name, Penuel, means "face of God." Anna, fulfilling the legacy of her father's name, is led to see the face of God in Jesus. Intriguing. The Holy Spirit illumines her inner eye to recognize God's glory in His Son, as the Scriptures beautifully put it: "For God, who said, 'Let light shine out of darkness,' made his light shine in our hearts to give us the light of the knowledge of God's glory displayed in the face of Christ" (2 Corinthians 4:6). She does not hesitate to reveal this newly discovered treasure. Anna "spoke about the child to all who were looking forward to the redemption of Jerusalem."

The Lord pairs and equally yokes Anna with Simeon in this account. Together they foreshadow the New Testament's liberating truth: "There is neither Jew nor Gentile, neither slave nor free, nor is there male and female, for you are all one in Christ Jesus" (Galatians 3:28). Both of them, through their almost-finished lives, present the crossover to a new time and era in the history of humankind.

Prayer

My loving God, I recognize the feebleness of my own strength to live a life of great devotion. Draw me into the intimacy of prayer and fasting under the guidance of the Holy Spirit. Amen.

Your Response

What is your desire for intimacy with God? Share this desire with Him in prayer and as you journal.

Lovingly,
Your friends

Are You Following Your Star?

Dear Fellow Seeker,

Have you ever searched for something or someone so intently that it cost you dearly in time and resources? You would not be deterred until you found what you had been searching for. Today we get a glimpse into what this journey of discovery was like for the Magi. Perhaps, as you read the text, you will discover your own hunger to search and to find Jesus in this season. Open your heart, body, mind, and resources to this discovery as you pray and study.

Preparing to Reflect

In Luke 15:8–10 we read the parable of the lost coin. A woman is relentless and inexhaustible in her search for this coin. Before I pray today, can I imagine being this treasure that God is specifically searching for? I approach my prayer time with this image in mind.

Prayer

My loving God, I would not know how and what to search for if it were not for Your burning desire for me. I thank You that, if I search for You with my whole heart, I will find You. Amen.

Story of the Day

After Jesus was born in Bethlehem in Judea, during the time of King Herod, Magi from the east came to Jerusalem and asked, "Where is the one who has been born king of the Jews? We saw his star when it rose and have come to worship him" (Matthew 2:1–2).

Entering the Scene

Most likely, the Magi are having an ordinary day, when suddenly an exclamation pierces their monotony, "Come and see!" All of their eyes are nailed to this one phenomenon in the sky. The sign is so powerful, significant, and unusual that it suspends each person's breath in an eternal moment.

Yes, the sign points to Judah, a country of historical opposition, and the star shows that the new King will be more significant than their own king. However, these gifted and knowledgeable astrologers let this Wonder transcend all political, cultural, and religious barriers because it is simply incomparable. The shifting in the atmosphere and their hearts causes them to refocus and launch their pursuit of the One to whom they long to give their devotion regardless of their own nobleness. No one and nothing holds them back.

They pack all that is needed. Their awareness and spiritual farsightedness impel them to bring gold, frankincense, and myrrh: symbols of divinity, worship, and anointing for someone's death. Astonishing. What and who originates this prophetic wisdom? Why does God lead these Gentile men to journey to Bethlehem?

Their single-mindedness and burning curiosity propel them toward an arduous and sometimes dangerous journey of many miles. We are struck by their relentless search and pureness of intent as we watch their caravans moving by day and night.

Come and watch with us for a moment! What do you notice about these men? What draws your eye and engages your heart? What might you learn about yourself if you were on this journey with them?

Going Deeper

The Magi remind us of the Emmaus story. Two disciples are walking on the road, Jesus joins them, but they don't recognize that it is He. When the eyes of their hearts are opened at the end, they exclaim, "Did not our hearts burn within us while He talked?" (Luke 24:13–32). Likewise, the Magi simply follow one guiding light, but their burning hearts do not fully understand the historical significance of this journey. None of them could have guessed that their journey would be written about in the Scriptures or that they would be the first in the Gentile world to worship the Savior.

So many parallels emerge between their lives and ours. Do we have the complete perception of what is transpiring now or will transpire long after we are gone? Not really. The undercurrent of God's intentions is often hidden to our everyday eye. We are solely called to be in touch with our burning hearts and follow them in humble obedience.

Have you ever simply followed your burning heart and been astoundingly surprised where it took you? Is your heart burning now? Is there a star out there calling your name and inviting you to follow it? It might flicker and not always be clearly visible. You might end up detouring like the wise men in Jerusalem, but a determined and faithful heart always detects the star again.

Prayer for the Journey

"Inspire me in all my decisions, and never let me neglect any of your inspirations." [Jacques Philippe, *In the School of the Holy Spirit*] Amen.

Your Response
Are any good pursuits calling your name? If yes, how are you going to act upon them? Does the flame of your heart need God's rekindling? Journal and pray.

Praying for God's direction in your life,
Liena and Jacqueline

_____

_____

_____

_____

_____

_____

_____

_____

_____

_____

_____

_____

_____

_____

_____

_____

_____

_____

_____

_____

_____

_____

_____

_____

Am I Stuck or Searching?

Greetings to You,

Have you ever had a guest who surprised you without a warning and whose message or impact changed your life? The wise men's arrival in Jerusalem rattle the city and bring forth some intriguing responses. Who are they? What might we learn from this story? Come and enter Jerusalem with us.

Preparing to Reflect

Many times Jesus dismissed the crowds in order to find a quiet place for communion with the Father in prayer. What crowds my internal life this season? Can I dismiss for even a little while my preoccupying thoughts and emotions to have an intentional time with my heavenly Father? I close my eyes for a moment and still my heart.

Prayer

Loving Father, fill me with all wisdom and understanding of Your Word for me today. Amen.

Story of the Day

When King Herod heard this he was disturbed, and all Jerusalem with him. When he had called together all the people's chief priests and teachers of the law, he asked them where the Messiah was to be born. "In Bethlehem in Judea," they replied, "for this is what the prophet has written:

> *'But you, Bethlehem, in the land of Judah,*
> *are by no means least among the rulers of Judah;*
> *for out of you will come a ruler*
> *who will shepherd my people Israel.'"*

Then Herod called the Magi secretly and found out from them the exact time the star had appeared. He sent them to Bethlehem and said, "Go and search carefully for the child. As soon as you find him, report to me, so that I too may go and worship him" (Matthew 2:3–8).

Entering the Scene

Where would you look for a king? Of course, the capitol; however, in this case, it turns out to be the wrong destination. The well-meaning wise men find themselves in Jerusalem in the audience of Herod only to learn that the Messiah would be born in Bethlehem. They proceed with human logic, only to discover God's "uncommon" sense.

The innocent searching of the Magi disturbs the entire city. Herod feels threatened; his paranoia spreads like wildfire. The chain of gossip unites all of Jerusalem in intrigue. Though many sense alarm, no one embarks upon a journey to meet the Messiah.

Even the scribes, who have studied the Scriptures for ages in order to identify the circumstances of the Messiah's advent, do not act upon the ancient knowledge and information from the Magi. They don't budge even an inch. The learned know everything, yet not enough to propel them to search for the Savior. The dots don't get connected and the knowledge in itself does not serve them in the least. They are so near but ironically so far from the Truth.

The wise men have come a long distance, but they are nearest to uncovering the Truth. Their knowing united with their burning hearts is a witness to a living faith. While all of Jerusalem stays stuck and boils in their own gossip, the wise men, who are Gentiles, freely travel on. "So the last will be first, and the first will be last" (Matthew 20:16).

Going Deeper

Fear and jealousy make us prisoners in the home of our own hearts. Because of it, Herod only sees in the Messiah a threat to himself. He does not see anything greater or unrelated to earthly kingdoms. The king's nearsightedness blinds him.

But it's not only Herod. Let's be honest with ourselves. When God brings someone great and amazing into our lives, how often do we not allow that person to become everything they could be for us and for themselves? We hinder their way because we don't see the greater good and we get caught up in our ego story. This leads to aborting our own growth and potentially great relationships due to either jealousy or insecurity. We witness our own nearsightedness in the context of friendships, intimate relationships, work, political, and even international affairs. Only maturity and humble confidence allows the strength of the other to fully blossom in our lives.

Prayer for the Journey

Our Father, help me to cross the boundaries of my own ego in reaching for Your highest good for all people. Amen.

Your Response

What does the response of Herod and the townspeople to the wise men stir up in you? We invite you to express your heart to the Lord or journal your observations.

Grace and peace,
Liena and Jacqueline

You Are Welcomed Now!

Dear Pilgrim,

Have you ever done the almost impossible and unreasonable just to be with someone special even for a brief moment? The Magi undertake just that kind of devoted, extreme quest. They make a journey over a "thousand hills": searching, overcoming, and giving up years of their lives just for a glimpse of the King and a moment of worship. How precious and treasured true adoration can be. Will you enter their celebration and find your own joy in Jesus' presence?

Preparing to Reflect

"The LORD delights in those who fear him, who put their hope in his unfailing love" (Psalm 147:11). I pause and cease from my daily responsibilities. I make a cup of a warm drink to relax and acknowledge the sacredness of this time. I delight in my Father and He delights in me.

Prayer

Lord, "Better is one day in your courts than a thousand elsewhere" (Psalm 84:10). I come to You to seek Your face and to drink from Your sweet presence. Amen.

Story of the Day

After they had heard the king, they went on their way, and the star they had seen when it rose went ahead of them until it stopped over the place where the child was. When they saw the star, they were overjoyed. On coming to the house, they saw the child with his mother Mary, and they bowed down and worshiped him. Then they opened their treasures and presented him with gifts of gold, frankincense and myrrh. And having been warned in a dream not to go back to Herod, they returned to their country by another route (Matthew 2:9-12).

Entering the Scene

The guiding star comes to rest; so do the Magi. Finally, the possibly two-year journey of pursuing, following, and prevailing is over. They eye one another in disbelief. Could this really be the end of their searching? Have they truly found the Holy One they have sought for so long?

Yes! They have found Him. They explode with joy like a Tour de France team who has finally crossed the finish line. We can almost hear their triumphant shouts of praise and see their excited dancing as they embrace each other.

They enter the abiding place of Jesus and His parents and bow at this miraculous sight. Jesus is most likely a toddler by now. They come and worship Him. Do you see a look of surprise on Mary's face? She is alone with the child and these strange men who speak a different language and bend their backs before her son. What are they muttering? What does this mean? More than that, they place these fancy, expensive gifts before Jesus. Does she even recognize what they are?

Despite all of the differences and what is not understood, we see people from vastly different worlds drawn together in one circle by the King of the Universe: Jesus. Is this the first ecumenical worship service ever? Imagine yourself among them. Join your worshipping to that of the Magi. How do you respond and express your delight?

Going Deeper

Why does God lead the Magi to find and worship Jesus? A parable in the Gospel of Luke gives insight into this mystery. Many guests are invited to a great banquet, but all find excuses. "The servant came back and reported this to his master. Then the owner of the house became angry and ordered his servant, 'Go out quickly into the streets and alleys of the town and bring in the poor, the crippled, the blind and the lame.'

"'Sir,' the servant said, 'what you ordered has been done, but there is still room.'

"Then the master told his servant, 'Go out to the roads and country lanes and compel them to come in, so that my house will be full. I tell you, not one of those who were invited will get a taste of my banquet'" (Luke 14:21–24).

Yes, it is true, Jesus "came to that which was his own, but his own did not receive him" (John 1:11). Now God has gathered a crowd of pagans to welcome His Son in this world. Jesus' own nation keeps quiet and "the stones" worship him in the form of the Magi. God always finds a way for Jesus to be glorified.

God also proclaims His love for all nations through the call of the Magi. The same door through which Jesus enters this world stays wide open to all people to pass through into His salvation. "This is good, and pleases God our Savior, who wants all people to be saved and to come to a knowledge of the truth" (1 Timothy 2:3–4). All are welcome.

It is so heartwarming to see that the expensive gifts from the pagans, the least expected people, are given to the holy family just before their escape to Egypt. We are sure they will benefit greatly from receiving each tribute to the majesty of this child King. The gifts are not only prophetic, but they also serve as the Father's provision for them.

Have there been times in your life when help has come not from the people you expected but from those least expected to extend their kindness, perhaps even total strangers? God's hand is not too short to use anyone or anything in our lives. "Taste and see that the LORD is good" (Psalm 34:8).

How do you think the Magi's lives have been changed by their encounter with Jesus? They have made a true spiritual pilgrimage and now return home with vibrant, singing hearts. How has this touched their servants, families, and friends? What do they say when they return home? We see their eyes forever fixed upon that star and following the life of Jesus, even from afar.

Prayer for the Journey

"Worthy is the Lamb, who was slain, to receive power and wealth and wisdom and strength and honor and glory and praise" (Revelation 5:12). Precious Jesus, lead me into unceasing worship of Your holy name. Amen.

Your Response

What part of the Magi's worship moved or inspired you? Journal and offer the movements of your heart to the Lord.

Celebrating Him,
Your devoted friends

Dream Messages:
Don't Dismiss Them and Miss Out

Greetings,

Dreams are such funny things. Jumbled images and messages and seemingly unrelated bits play across our minds in the night. Sometimes we wake up, wipe our eyes, shake our heads, and ask, "What did all of that mean?"

Yet, we know that God speaks to us through and in our dreams. Joseph knows this firsthand. Today's text recounts the story of Joseph receiving the command in a dream to take his family and flee to Egypt. What messages is God sending you in your dreams?

Preparing to Reflect

I rest in the space where I am seated. I close my eyes and take in a few deep breaths. How has God spoken to me lately? I remember with thanksgiving. I allow Him to open my mind and heart and to speak to me anew in this time of prayer.

Prayer

Lord, thank You for speaking to me in countless ways, including dreams. Give me a deeper understanding of Your messages to me today. Amen.

Story of the Day

When they had gone, an angel of the Lord appeared to Joseph in a dream. "Get up," he said, "take the child and his mother and escape to Egypt. Stay there until I tell you, for Herod is going to search for the child to kill him" (Matthew 2:13).

Entering the Scene

Have you ever been startled and awakened with news in the middle of night? "Get up, there is a flood. You need to leave your house!" "There is a fire! We need to evacuate you." "He died." "Come quickly, she is very sick." Most of us know this feeling.

Likewise, Joseph stares into the dark with his eyes wide open. His head spins as he tries to comprehend the directive given to him in the dream. "Get up, take the child and his mother. The king-murderer is after him." Where should he go?

The angel sends them not to a town nearby or a neighboring region but to a different country altogether. How do you see him awakening Mary with this news? It is as if a night visitor would awaken us with the command to walk to Mexico or another country with a little child in our arms. Can you see the hurry of their quick preparations? What do Mary and Joseph bring? Oh, the Magi's gifts. Are they the Father's gracious provision? He is always one step ahead of us.

Joseph leads his family without hesitation or many words. Does he find the angel's words strangely comforting and reassuring? God conveys the most important messages to Joseph in dreams, three times that we know of. There is a hard journey ahead of them, yet there is a promise of guidance. The angel promises another meeting with Joseph to direct his future steps. One can overcome the unfathomable with the assurance of companionship. How has this been true in your life?

Going Deeper

Does God have a favorite way of communicating with you? How does He usually get your attention? Is it that deep inner knowing, a soundless voice within you? Perhaps He uses Scripture, nature, dreams, or people around you? Think of a time when you knew beyond understanding that God was pointing you to go in a specific direction. What did you learn about God's way of speaking to you from that time?

There have been a few times when I, Liena, have been awakened from a dream with an internal tug for a certain action. Some years ago we opened our home to a man who was very ill and did not have a family. One day I was taking a nap and was awakened by a voice in a dream, "Go and talk to Gunars!"

Deep down I felt an invitation to speak to him about dying. I went to Gunars's room, sat on the edge of his bed, and plainly asked what he felt about passing away. This question ushered us into the most beautiful conversation about heaven, Christ's sacrifice, and the assurance of God's forgiveness and love. The light of peace gradually increased in his eyes to a full glow.

After our conversation, he asked me to help him go to the bathroom. When we were walking back, he needed to rest. We both sat on the floor, and I took him in my arms. As we were sitting there, his head against my chest, I realized he was dying. I gently stroked his head as his spirit joined the setting sun. The surpassing beauty and sacredness of this moment caused my heart to swell.

Later my mother and I cleaned, shaved, and dressed him in preparation for his burial. We put my wool socks on him, as Gunars was a poor man without any appropriate shoes. There were no other means but a wheelbarrow to use for Gunars's transportation to the church to keep him cool before his entombment. It was comical and grievous all at once. We laughed and cried as his body made funny postures while we pushed him to the destination. All our pains were outshined by the joy that this lonely man died knowing not only human love but God's love also.

The next night he came to my mother in her dream and said, "Thank you very much for everything you have done for me. I am doing very well, and by the way, those socks feel great!"

I am so glad I listened to the directive given to me in my dream. Quite often we dismiss simple inspirations, strong internal promptings, or that deep inner knowing that calls for action. When we dismiss these nudges from the Holy Spirit, we miss out. We pass up the most splendid opportunities.

This season invites us to recommit to a deeper way of listening followed by immediate obedience. "So he got up" . . . Joseph, our brother in the faith, leads us into a way of swift responsiveness.

Prayer for the Journey

Loving Abba, we so desire to be in sync with the Holy Spirit and Your guidance. Help us to move from dismissing You to perceiving Your heartbeat for us and for all humanity. Amen.

Your Response

How do you relate to Joseph and the story above? Is there any prayer arising in your heart in response to today's meditation? We invite you to pray and journal now.

Praying for God's guidance for you,
Liena and Jacqueline

Jesus—the Refugee

Dear Reader,

War and conflict rip lives apart. To protect their families and loved ones, people leave behind their countries, customs, and comforts and flee to a place of greater safety. The evening news puts faces and names to the people caught in the crossfire. Have you ever thought of Jesus as a refugee? Let's see how today's story opens up this reality for us.

Preparing to Reflect

"To pray is to listen, to move through my own chattering to God, to that place where I can be silent and listen to what God may have to say." [Madeleine L'Engle] Can I gently pass through all the chatter and draw my attention to that still center within me? I become aware of my breathing, and I still myself to listen to the voice of Love.

Prayer

Mighty and tender God, You are my hiding place. "Keep me as the apple of your eye; hide me in the shadow of your wings" (Psalm 17:8). Amen.

Story of the Day

So he got up, took the child and his mother during the night and left for Egypt, where he stayed until the death of Herod" (Matthew 2:14–15).

Entering the Scene

Upon God's call, Joseph and Mary escape from their own country with the Son of God in their arms. How does it feel to carry that precious responsibility?

It is a great distance from Bethlehem to the border of Egypt, the Roman province outside Herod's jurisdiction. If the holy family were headed further to Alexandria, where many Jews had found refuge, it would have been twice as long. What is that journey like for them in the heat of the day and the chill of the night? How do you see these refuges traveling as God leads them?

What awaits Mary, Joseph, and Jesus in Egypt? Every refugee wrestles with at least one of the following: belonging, homelessness, fear, hunger, sickness, death, being downgraded to the bottom of the social ladder, a new language, foreign traditions, keeping alive their own customs and faith practices, homesickness, and concerns about his or her loved ones at home.

Despite the many difficulties, God's promise remains faithful. "The LORD watches over the foreigner and sustains the fatherless and the widow" (Psalm 146:9). Has this been true in your own life or in the life of someone you know?

Going Deeper

An inseparable bond of deep compassion and identification between Jesus and refugees of all times continue to this very day. As we watch the holy family leaving their country, an image of Jesus, the refugee, walking among all of the exiled, emerges in our heart's awareness. He is one of them in solidarity of displacement, persecution, and suffering. We see Jesus, the Savior child, amongst all children born in the war zone, on the road, fleeing injustice.

This story also paints a very clear picture of Jesus' life not being privileged in any way, even from birth. He is one of us: familiar with being poor and outcast, acquainted with a refugee's life. Jesus chooses not to consider Himself entitled to anything in this world. He lives a life marked by emptying Himself. "Who, being in very nature God, did not consider equality with God something to be used to his own advantage; rather, he made himself nothing by taking the very nature of a servant, being made in human likeness" (Philippians 2: 6–7).

> Jesus had only one "operating mode." Everything he did, he did by self-emptying. He emptied himself and descended into human form. And he emptied himself still further ("even unto death on the cross") and fell through the bottom to return to the realms of dominion and glory. In whatever life circumstances, Jesus always responded with the same motion of self-emptying—or to put it another way, of the same motion of *descent*: going lower, taking the lower place, not the higher. [Cynthia Bourgeault, *The Wisdom Jesus*]

Jesus not only dies for us, but He also gives His life away, beginning with the miracle of the incarnation. He leaves His homeland of heaven. Being a refugee from His native land marks the beginning of His passion. He suffered many small, daily deaths all of His life so that we would gain the fullness of life.

Prayer for the Journey

Loving Jesus, thank You for teaching me that ascending in my spiritual life comes through descending in humility. Form in me Your heart. Amen.

Your Response

How does Jesus' refugee journey move you to pray? Open your heart to express yourself to God. Journal your thoughts.

May God's peace be yours,
Your sisters in Christ

Unspeakable Sacrifice

Shalom,

The harsh realities of life can be unsparing and chilling to the bone. Today's passage speaks of Herod's mass killing of children. Such devastation. Human pride can prompt us to commit heinous crimes. In order to open ourselves to this story, we need to be ready to open ourselves to our own shadow side.

Preparing to Reflect

Because of God's unconditional and absolute love, I can face my light and dark side with equal peace. God holds all of who I am with utmost tenderness.

How am I this day? What are the realities of my heart I want to bring to God in this time of prayer? I ponder for a moment and still myself before His healing love.

Prayer

Abba Father, I offer myself to You today. Help me to see my human brokenness through You this day. Amen.

Story of the Day

When Herod realized that he had been outwitted by the Magi, he was furious, and he gave orders to kill all the boys in Bethlehem and its vicinity who were two years old and under, in accordance with the time he had learned from the Magi. Then what was said through the prophet Jeremiah was fulfilled:

> *"A voice is heard in Ramah,*
> > *weeping and great mourning,*
> *Rachel weeping for her children*
> > *and refusing to be comforted,*
> *because they are no more" (Matthew 2:16–18).*

Entering the Scene

"They have outwitted me! How dare they?" Herod succumbs to insane limits of paranoia once again. He has already killed a couple of his own sons and one of his wives. Now he is going after these innocent souls.

Bellows of pride arise within him and swell into pure rage. His soldiers get the order to kill all the baby boys under two years old in Bethlehem and the surrounding region. How much has one hardened his heart to be able to pierce a sword through a baby's body?

Chaos, people running, holding on to their living and dying children, covering the bodies of their young with their own bodies, screaming, crying, praying, and cursing all at once. How could this be happening?

Going Deeper

The existence of evil and satanic forces is undeniably woven into the fabric of these events. How can one deny this? Hell is panicked and outraged by the birth of the Messiah and desperately uses any one of its servants to lash out against God and His people. In this case, Herod falls into the snare of evil. We see unquestionable war between the forces of light and darkness as witnessed many times before and since in the history of humankind.

It is not easy to hear Christ's words, "If they persecuted Me, they will also persecute you . . . because they do not know the One who sent Me" (John 15:20–21 NASB).

Most of us have heard the saying "freedom is never free." So it is with our salvation. Christ pays the price for our freedom, and with Him all the martyrs of the faith. Before the gospel of salvation ever reached you and me, multitudes of souls paved the way by sacrificing their very lives. These innocent children, victims of violence, were the first to pay for our redemption. How priceless and precious is the ultimate gift of life.

Pause for a moment in appreciation and gratitude for every life given on your behalf. What will you do with this treasure? How will the way you live your life reflect the price paid for you?

Prayer for the Journey
Father, my heart grieves; I am simply silent and grateful. Thank You. Amen.

Your Response
What is your heart's response to today's Scripture reading? Offer God your questions and reflections in prayer or writing.

Prayerfully,
Liena and Jacqueline

185

Refusing to Be Comforted

God's Child,

It would be hard to find a human heart that has not been bruised, cracked, and shaped by grief. So many of us have wrestled with grief in the same way that Jacob wrestled with God. Is there a possibility of coming out blessed on the other side? Come and delve into this with us.

Preparing to Reflect

"What no eye has seen, what no ear has heard, and what no human mind has conceived"—the things God has prepared for those who love him" (1 Corinthians 2:9).

"We honor God the most by letting Him love us. Would you let Him love you?" [Max Lucado]

Can I open my heart and let God love me during this time of prayer? Can I expect the inconceivable for just one moment?

Prayer

Holy Trinity, teach me the art of being loved and the art of returning that love to You and this world. Amen.

Story of the Day

> *"A voice is heard in Ramah,*
> *weeping and great mourning,*
> *Rachel weeping for her children*
> *and refusing to be comforted,*
> *because they are no more" (Matthew 2:18).*

Entering the Scene

The communal grief erupts and the "volcanic ashes" are seen even after many decades. Men and women rip their clothing and the sea of lamentation washes over their town. Allow this grief to wash over you. People around you sit in sackcloth while sprinkling ashes and dust on their heads. Sounds of weeping and wailing envelope you. Remain in the middle of town; observe and feel this grief. What is it like for you?

People of Bethlehem, drunk with sorrow, stagger to each other's homes to comfort and hold each other and to mourn together. After the funerals, women gather around their children's graves early in the morning to lament, sob, and chant their prayers. Does this remind you of anything you have experienced in your lifetime? The mass shootings and acts of terrorism that have spread like wildfire across our country and the world come to our minds.

The prophetic words pulsate with strength: even Rachel, the spiritual mother of Israel, who is buried in Ramah next to Bethlehem, refuses to be comforted.

Going Deeper

Have you ever refused to be consoled: that place in your grief where you preferred searing pain to sure and certain comfort? At times, we find ourselves in this maelstrom of emotions; nursing our mourning seems to preserve the memory of the lost loved one. If we loosen our grip on our pain and reach out to receive comfort, we feel we will also lose what is left to us of the person who is gone.

In the six months following my mother's death, I, Jacqueline, pitched a tent in "Camp No Comfort." The stronger the pangs of grief, the more I felt she was present to me. This thought seems irrational to me now, yet I know that we cannot expect ourselves to be rational in those moments.

Slowly, oh so slowly, I began to see that the Lord would put women into my life who nurtured me as my mother would have. A very dear friend, Betty Rushing, stood with me through the months of my cancer treatment in such a loving way. She was the one who heard my tears as I called to tell her of the pain of losing my hair. Being nurtured in a motherly way has also been as simple as another friend bringing me my favorite cookie that my mom used to bake at Christmas.

Every spring, I do my best to plant pansies as my mother did, and on her birthday, I eat Mexican food (her favorite!). More recently, I have adopted a little girl to pass on the gift of love that my mother gave to me. I have had to make a conscious choice to be comforted. In this process, God restores me and makes me whole again in places that I thought would forever have a gaping hole.

Truly "there is a season for everything under the sun," as the wise Solomon expressed. There is a time to grieve and there is a time to cross the bridge to allowing oneself to be comforted and restored.

Prayer for the Journey
Holy Spirit, there is no greater Comforter than You. Teach me to reap the full benefit of what You give so freely to me. Amen.

Your Response

In what ways or in which circumstances do you need to choose to be comforted? Take this verse to heart and journal your thoughts: "Praise be to the God and Father of our Lord Jesus Christ, the Father of compassion and the God of all comfort" (2 Corinthians 1:3).

Be safe beneath His wings,
Your friends in Jesus

A Seed of Promise

Christ's Beloved,

Like Joseph while he was in Egypt, we all carry the ordinary burdens of everyday living. But what makes this load light and our hearts joyful as we travel on life's path? Joseph carried God's promises, which were like a seed pushing up through the ground of his heart and flourishing with hope into his everyday life. Do you need to reconnect to any of God's promises given to you? Let today's Scripture guide you.

Preparing to Reflect

The link between God and ourselves established when we pray is also a basic element of stability in our lives. God is the Rock, whose love is unshakable, "the Father of light with whom there is no shadow or variation due to change" (Jas 1:17). . . . Prayer teaches us to put down our roots in God, to "abide in his love" (Jn 15:9), to find strength and security in him, thus empowering us in turn to become stable supports for others. [Jacques Philippe, *Thirsting for Prayer*]

Before I pray, I take a deep appreciative breath of God's unchanging nature. I let go of my concerns and rest in God's stability and love for I am here to be nurtured.

Prayer

Thank You, loving God, for being my Rock whose love is unshakable and unchangeable. Only with You I can wait well through the tempests of life. Amen.

Story of the Day

After Herod died, an angel of the Lord appeared in a dream to Joseph in Egypt and said, "Get up, take the child and his mother and go to the land of Israel, for those who were trying to take the child's life are dead."

So he got up, took the child and his mother and went to the land of Israel (Matthew 2:19–20).

Entering the Scene

Joseph goes about his daily living, falling and rising under the misery of a refugee life while taking care of his family. However, in the midst of his life as an expatriate, we also imagine moments of deep joy: catching the smile on his child's face, a caress from his wife, or the beauty of the natural world around him. In the background of daily living the angel's words echo with the utmost sound of promise: "Stay there until I tell you" (Matthew 2:13). Isn't it this kind of hope that keeps all of us going?

What is your specific hope and God's promise that sustains you on a daily basis?

God remembers Joseph in the same way He remembered the Israelites. God speaks once again to him in a dream: "Get up, take the child and his mother and go to the land of Israel." Does Joseph weep tears of joy upon receiving this message? How do you imagine Mary expressing her joy when hearing the good news from Joseph? They are led back to their own land just as Israel was led out of Egypt long ago. The prophecy is sealed: "Out of Egypt I called my son" (Matthew 2:15).

Going Deeper

Advent, and so much about our lives, is about waiting for the fulfillment of God's promises. There are so many people in the Bible who spend the majority of their lives in a state of waiting. Just think of the ones we have companioned with so far: Zechariah, Elizabeth, Mary, Simeon, Anna, Joseph, and Israel as a whole.

It is crucial to understand that the waiting of these devoted believers is never done in a vacuum. Their waiting is always in response to God's promises and not merely a wish. Waiting is an extension of what God has done in their lives already.

> People who wait have received a promise that allows them to wait. They have received something that is at work within them, like a seed that has started to grow. This is very important. We can only really wait if what we are waiting for has already begun for us. So waiting is never a movement from nothing to something. It is always a movement from something to something more. [Henri J. M. Nouwen, *The Path of Waiting*]

Joseph is a great example: he patiently waits for the continuation of the work God had already begun.

As we examine our lives, what is that "something" that God has already initiated in your life? Has there been a strong impression or a promise? Is there something God is waiting for in your life that is stalling the fulfillment of the promise? Maybe certain steps need to be taken towards the assurance given to you. The birth of a promise takes both: the courage of a free heart and God's timing.

Prayer for the Journey

Loving Trinity, show me the next step toward Your promise in my life and teach me to receive the long awaited gifts in a free and nonattached way. Amen.

Your Response

How does God invite you to respond to today's passage? Talk to Him about the stirrings in your heart and journal.

Rest in His promises,
Your companions

Strength, Grace, and Wisdom

Dear Friend,

What are the landmarks for our deepening life with God? In the everyday moments of life, we may have difficulty pointing out this growth. In our story today, we see the very human side of Jesus: His physical, emotional, and spiritual maturation. What does this look like for Him? Let's take a peek.

Preparing to Reflect

"There are very few people who realize what God would make of them if they abandoned themselves into his hands, and let themselves be formed by his grace" (St. Ignatius). What invitation do I hear in these words? Can I, at this moment, leave aside my preoccupations and intentionally place myself into God's hands to be formed by His touch and infused with His wisdom?

Prayer

"Teach us to number our days, that we may gain a heart of wisdom" (Psalm 90:12). Amen.

Story of the Day

When Joseph and Mary had done everything required by the Law of the Lord, they returned to Galilee to their own town of Nazareth. And the child grew and became strong; he was filled with wisdom, and the grace of God was on him (Luke 2:39–40).

Entering the Scene

What sense do you get from reading this story? We taste the delicious fruit of peace that follows the obedience of Mary and Joseph. After Jesus' dedication at the temple, they faithfully resume their daily duties. You can hear the heartbeat of the daily rhythm: rising with the sun, working, raising a child, preparing meals, resting, attending to each other, interacting with the community, and worship. It's so plain and simple, but underneath it all, the extraordinary person of Jesus is formed.

His parents grow along with him. Jean-Pierre de Caussade would call it "the sacrament of the present moment." The whole essence of the spiritual life consists in surrendering one's being to God and then being responsive to His shaping of us under the disguise of daily life and duties. Ordinary living becomes a sacrament by keeping in step with the Holy Spirit. How do you experience the sacrament of the present moment? Can you identify with Jesus who, draped in the Father's favor, grows into His identity one ordinary day at time?

Going Deeper

What is the essence of our true growth and formation as it is seen in Jesus? Three words draw our attention: *strength*, *wisdom*, and *grace*. Let's look closer at them.

The word *strength* in Greek is translated as "staunch in spirit." This implies that a person exudes loyalty, faithfulness, steadfastness, and deep devotion. Proverbs 9:10 says that the fear of the Lord, holy awe and reverence, is the beginning of wisdom. Those are the roots that keep deepening in Jesus as He keeps advancing as a person.

Along with the rootedness, wisdom keeps increasing at the core of His very being. It is very significant that knowledge is not mentioned here nor in other texts referring to His formation.

What is wisdom? Who do you consider to be a truly wise person in your life? We love to think that wisdom comprises a spiritual way of knowing and insight that transcends rational understanding. For bread to rise, the flour has to be mixed with yeast; and for true wisdom to emerge, the knowing that comes through our minds, hearts, bodies, nature, and experiences has to be mixed with the Spirit. This is why the third component, grace, is so essential for true growth.

Grace is the active presence of God that also can be thought of as His favor being at work. Everything that comes to Jesus in His life passes through the Spirit, and that is what makes Him a wise and well-formed man.

Are staunchness of the inner man, wisdom, and grace the focus of spiritual formation in your faith community and in your personal life? This is our true Epiphany challenge.

Prayer for the Journey

Lord, we remember Your pleasure over Solomon's prayer for a wise and discerning heart. We join him in our desire for a life of true wisdom, strength, and favor. Amen.

Your Response

How do you react to the fact that Jesus needed to grow as we do? In what areas would you like to grow in this coming year? Pray and journal your intentions.

Manifold blessings,
Liena and Jacqueline

Continual Epiphany

Dear Friend,

Every good-bye holds a promise of hello to new experiences and discoveries. We hope that a seed of spiritual curiosity has been planted in your heart while reading our letters to you. We pray that you would continue your fellowship with God on a daily basis leading you to your own epiphanies. To encourage you we would like to share how this devotional came about and how you can delve into Scriptures on your own or with someone close to you.

Jacqueline and I have been friends for over a decade. Our friendship has been the most precious gift bestowed upon us. A couple of years ago, we decided to take time every week to pray together. In the beginning we prayed in person during a Christmas vacation that we shared together. Later, after Jacqueline returned home, we prayed faithfully over the phone. We discovered that St. Ignatius's prayer method (*The Spiritual Exercises of St. Ignatius)* was the most helpful tool for our time in prayer.

Here are the steps we take each time we pray together:

Preparing to Reflect and Pray

We choose a Bible text and start with a brief silence and recollection of ourselves before the presence of God.

Seeking the Holy Spirit's Guidance

Jacqueline and I ask the Holy Spirit to illuminate the Scriptures and our own hearts.

Engaging the Imagination

We slowly read the Scriptures for the first time and use all our senses to enter the scene depicted in the passage. We allow God to use our imagination to connect with the real life of His word. Jacqueline and I discuss what we feel and perceive.

Engaging the Heart and Intellect

Next we read the Scriptures slowly for the second time and pay attention to words, phrases, and God's deeper message to us. We share our impressions with each other.

Praying the Scriptures

We pray very specifically for the new revelations to take root in our hearts and shape our lives. We permit the Scriptures to form our prayers. "One of the lovely things about the Bible is that God not only addresses us, speaking to our hearts, but also gives us words in which to respond." [Jacques Philippe, *Thirsting for Prayer*]

The greatest adventure of all is into the heart of God. We hope that you will find a travelling companion to accompany you and the Holy Spirit. Have a most delightful and life transforming journey!

With deepest gratitude,
Liena and Jacqueline

P.S. For speaking engagements and book sales at your church before Advent or any other comments and request, please, email sharinginjoy@ gmail.com. Thank you.

www.lienasgifts.com
www.adventtoepiphany.com